T0065203

THE HISTORY OF THE PROGRESSIVE MOVEMENT IN THE UNITED STATES AND HOW LIBERALISM HAS CREATED A MEDIOCRE SOCIETY

THE HISTORY OF THE PROGRESSIVE MOVEMENT IN THE UNITED STATES AND HOW LIBERALISM HAS CREATED A MEDIOCRE SOCIETY

RALPH E SAUCIER

THE HISTORY OF THE PROGRESSIVE MOVEMENT IN THE UNITED STATES AND HOW LIBERALISM HAS CREATED A MEDIOCRE SOCIETY

iUniverse books may be ordered through booksellers or by contacting:

iUniverse
1663 Liberty Drive
Bloomington, IN 47403
www.iuniverse.com
844-349-9409

ISBN: 978-1-6632-2964-9 (sc)
ISBN: 978-1-6632-2998-4 (hc)
ISBN: 978-1-6632-2965-6 (e)

Print information available on the last page.

iUniverse rev. date: 09/29/2021

DISCLAIMER: As you read this book you will find many quotes and paragraphs from many writers, presidential libraries, and quotes taken off the internet, some or all of which may or may not have been attributed to the original author. This author does not claim that any of these quotes and paragraphs came from this author, and he does not claim any of his self-thoughts as being his writings and quotes from these events or publications. The author does have many of his thoughts in this writing, having had many years on a political town committee, having been a town campaign manager for a prominent state representative, and has had many years of knowledge in the political atmosphere of the country. Having have been born in the 40's and seen the change in the political atmosphere and policies over the years, it is felt by this author that his years in politics have given him sufficient credentials to write about the changes that have occurred since the start of the progressiveness in the country.

CONTENTS

INTRODUCTION

The Mediocre Society of Today:
<u>Is American Broken?</u>

Webster describes Mediocre as: "**mediocre** - moderate to inferior in quality." Joseph Heller in Catch 22 says, ""Some men are born mediocre, some men achieve mediocrity, and some people have mediocre thrust upon them." At the time of George Washington, every man and woman knew what they had to do and how they had to perform to survive. How is that different from today?

It seems that we, in our society today, don't seem to understand where we came from, what our heritage represents and where we are going to end up! This will not be a long narrative but a simple book to understand the slave mentality we have put ourselves into with the politicians we have put in office, from George Washington to the present. I have read the life story of George Washington, John Adams, Thomas Jefferson, John Kennedy, who were our first three presidents and a Democratic President who I believe was a greater conservative than Democrats that we have in office today. After all, President Kennedy cut taxes for both individuals and corporations to create a vigorous economy. I thought it was worth looking into what these Presidents tried to do in order for the average American to have the freedom that they wanted.

The idea of this book is to look at the Presidents since George Washington and watch the progressive change through the last 200 years to where we have a socialistic entitlement state. A socialist state is where the individual does not feel he needs to earn what he needs for survival; that the government will provide it for him. What is entitlement? *[Webster's Dictionary]* says,

a. the condition of having a right to have, do, or get something.
b. the feeling or belief that you deserve to be given something (such as special privileges); and
c. a type of financial help provided by the government for members of a particular group.

{Author's Note: If you put "mediocre" and "entitlement" together, are we describing a particular segment of society? Are there people who are living in poverty of their own choosing because of government programs that put them in a situation that they feel they have a right to the assistance, or they deserve this financial assistance from the government? Where did this feeling come from? And most of all, what is being done to correct it, if anything. I am asking a lot of questions here and I hope to answer them by studying and analyzing our Presidents and where it all began and where it is today.

What happens to the people receiving the entitlement -- when does it stop? And it has to. As in our home budgets, and like my father used to say to me, "Ralph, you can't make $1.00 and spend $2.00." As of this writing the United States of American has a deficit of over $16.5 trillion.}

In fiscal year 2012, the federal government spent $3.5 trillion, amounting to 23 percent of the nation's Gross Domestic Product (GDP). Of that $3.5 trillion, nearly $2.5 trillion was financed by federal revenues. The remaining amount (about $1.1 trillion) was financed by borrowing; this deficit will ultimately be paid for by future taxpayers – our children and grandchildren; and perhaps even our great-grandchildren. As the graph on the next page shows, three major areas of spending each make up about one-fifth of the budget: *[Congressional Budget Office: An Update to the Budget and Economic Outlook: Fiscal Years 2012 to 2022]*

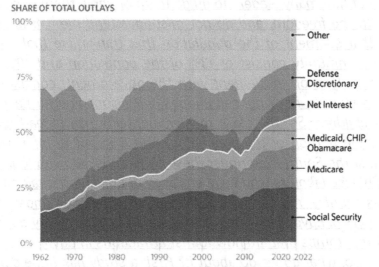

Entitlements and Interest Are Crowding Out Other Spending

SHARE OF TOTAL OUTLAYS

- Other
- Defense Discretionary
- Net Interest
- Medicaid, CHIP, Obamacare
- Medicare
- Social Security

100%

75%

50%

25%

0%

1962 1970 1980 1990 2000 2010 2020 2022

Sources: Congressional Budget Office, *An Update to the Economic and Budget Outlook: Fiscal Years 2012 to 2022*, Table 1-1, http://cbo.gov/publication/43543 (accessed August 23, 2012), and Office of Management and Budget, *Budget of the U.S. Government, FY 2013: Historical Tables*, Table 8.5, February 2012, http://www.whitehouse.gov/omb/budget/Historicals (accessed August 8, 2012).

Federal Spending by the Numbers 2012 ☎ heritage.org

{Author's Note: So how close are we to bankruptcy? Entitlement programs account for approximately 62% of the Federal Budget. Of that 22% is health care and Medicare Programs, 21% is Social Security, and 19% is welfare and other entitlement such as food stamps; etc. I feel that Social Security is an earned retirement by the senior citizens and definitely should not be considered entitlement. Since approximately 31% of our budget is borrowed (you might say from unfriendly countries, such as China) surely, we could cut a good chunk out of this before we go bankrupt.

Before we start analyzing this entitlement/slave mentality that I am describing, let us again understand that this did not happen overnight. Yes, recent politicians have made it worse, and I believe they want to make the United States a Socialist country so they can control the population. This sounds too familiar; who has tried that in the 20th Century and failed? What many groups do not understand is that the slave mentality of the South before the Civil War and years after has only switched to who is the master! Abraham Lincoln may have freed the slaves, but they have not had many leaders to guide them or show them what to do with the freedom, and do not misunderstand me -- it is not only that segment of the population that thinks like that. The Black community consist of 13% of the population and 49% is on some type of entitlement with the government, consisting of food stamps, housing, cell phones, televisions and for having more children. So, the slave master mentality has spread to a very large portion of the population. And it is not to infer here that just the South lived under these conditions. You can look at the Chinese laborers who were enslaved in building the railroads in this country. You can look at the Jewish population under the Pharaoh's of Egypt. How they were enslaved to build the Pyramids and other tombs that are now tourist attractions in Egypt.

So, what do we do about it? First, a study has to be done of where the mentality of dependency on the government for this entitlement came from. This has to be done before we can understand how to fix it. The question can also be asked, where do the churches fit into this? Years ago, in the startup of the country, the churches were the morality builders for the people. The pastors, priests, etc. guided the people on what was right and wrong. But they have chickened out and left the morality judgment to the government. One important thing to remember in reading this is that it is not intended to single out a particular segment of the population, but to use it as an analysis of how it was in our country's early years and compare the "master" then to what is going on with our socialism and the "masters" sitting in a different white house. The inspiration to write this came from my upbringing in the 50's and 60's and as I said to my wife, "Our grandchildren will never know the freedom we had and how great the country was at that time." Government intervention was minimal, and policeman were our friends. You did not have to fear authority, it was a time when kids took responsibility for what they did, so authority was more understanding and more tolerant of minor incidents.

Many Conservatives and Republicans like to say that the Progressive movement was a Democratic idea, and that Woodrow

Wilson was the start of it all. Although he contributed to it, let us not forget President Theodore Roosevelt. He became disenchanted with President Howard Taft because President Taft did not follow the policies of President Roosevelt. Before that they were great friends and this non-progressive movement that President Taft had did not fit well with Theodore Roosevelt.

Roosevelt felt that the middle class should have a chance in life and had a strong feeling for them. Although his Progressiveness was, some might say, intended to tame down the government and give the citizens a fair shake in life and to protect them from big business or even the government.}

CHAPTER 1

Theodore Roosevelt
The New Nationalism

Theodore Roosevelt (1858-1919) was the 26th president of the United States and a proponent of the "New Nationalist" variety of Progressivism. A master of populist rhetoric and public charm, Roosevelt quickly tapped into the widespread favor for reform. His administration pursued some widely publicized antitrust cases against large companies like Northern Securities and the Swift Beef Trust, but for all his aggressive rhetoric, Roosevelt actually went after fewer monopolies than his successor, William Howard Taft. *[BRIA 23 1 b Progressives and the Era of Trustbusting— Constitutional Rights Foundation – Bill of Rights in Action (Spring of 2007 Volume 23, No.1]*

The economy between the years of 1900-1914 was one of prosperity. The Progressivism movement of that period helped enhance that prosperity. There were problems, and all did not seem like it was on the surface. There was urban poverty, poor working conditions, and high accident rates. The rich were getting richer faster than the poor got richer. Banks became very important because they were able to float big loans assisting big business to consolidate and become larger. To protect investments, they wanted control of enterprises. J.P. Morgan is a good example. Bigness has advantages but bankers are not always innovative or receptive to new ideas. They were not concerned with working conditions, or even the environment.

Roosevelt was the first president to involve the federal government in protecting and preserving the environment. As a boy, "Teddy" had planned to grow up to be a biologist or zoologist; animals and birds fascinated him. As an adult, he had owned and operated a ranch and had hunted big game in Africa. Roosevelt loved the outdoors and the natural wilderness and was determined to use his authority as president to protect it. Roosevelt created many National Parks which, as we know, if he did not the environment would have continued to be abused. He felt that these parks had to be created so our children and their children would know and appreciate the beauty of America. I, for one, feel that President Roosevelt is best known for this and should be credited for saving the beauty of America, since President Roosevelt is known for creating The National Park Service.

The Progressives also involved themselves in political reform and were determined to give the voters of America a greater voice in their own government. Roosevelt's intention was to wipe out the big-city political machines. Voters also complained about national politics, feeling that their senators and congressmen were nothing more than the slaves and puppets of the big business owners who had paid so much money to get them elected.

The first step the Progressives took was to fight for reform on the local level, where voters selected delegates who nominated candidates for office. Progressives supported the direct primary, in which voters cast their votes directly for the candidates. Between 1902 and 1916, most states switched to a direct-primary system.

The Constitution granted the citizens the right to elect their representatives in Congress directly—but only those in the House of Representatives. Those in the Senate were chosen by the state legislatures. In 1913, thanks to Progressive efforts, the Seventeenth Amendment established direct popular election of senators. This helped eliminate the political popularity of who went to the Senate owing someone for the appointment.

The Progressives also fought for a secret, uniform ballot. At that time, political parties printed their own ballots in different colors, so that anyone could see how anyone else was voting. This made it easy for the precinct captains and any representative of a powerful vested interest to identify anyone not voting the way they wanted him to. This open voting system made intimidation easy; few voters wanted to risk retaliation by displeasing any strong-arm interests. With a uniform ballot, voting would be private and secret. By 1910, most states had bowed to Progressive pressure and converted to a secret ballot.

Progressives also believed that the people needed a mechanism by which they could propose or reject legislation on the state level. In Osawatomie, Kansas, on August 31, 1910 Roosevelt talked about three measures, all supported by the Progressives that would make this possible. By 1916, most states had adopted all three which were:

1. Human welfare was more important over property rights.
2. A powerful Federal government could regulate the economy and guarantee justice.
3. The concentration of industry was a natural part of the economy.

Some middle-class Americans began backing away from the Progressive movement because they felt it was almost too successful. Its goal had been to help the working class, but some middle-class Americans did not want working-class lives improved too much. They did not want the lower classes to gain too much political or economic power, because they felt this would threaten their own position. This is a major theme throughout all human history -- a class with power always feels threatened when the classes below it begins to acquire power of their own.

We need to understand that most of the Progressiveness that President Roosevelt fought for was more for political reform: to give the citizens more of a voice in their government; environmental change to protect America and its wildlife; to create parks and create the Forest Service to help protect the parks. President Roosevelt believed that the middle class was equal and should be treated equal by lowering the working week hours from 16 hours per day to 10. His Progressive movement was not a burden but was a help to Americans. It did not necessarily end up in the American citizen paying less taxes, but it was taking more money out of the middle working-class wages. President Roosevelt and President Taft, who succeeded President Roosevelt, who were both Republicans, had a totally different philosophy than President Wilson, who many believe was the "Father of the Progressive Movement" and who became President after President Taft.

As president, Theodore Roosevelt had to deal with the dominant conservative wing of his party and a Congress hostile to reform. He took the reins of the presidency without much more of a plan than to emulate Abraham Lincoln's wisdom and his ability to unite the nation. But legislation required the cooperation of Congress, and it was not readily won. T.R.'s legislative victories were modest but historic -- a railroad regulation bill, a Meat Inspection Act, and a Pure Food and Drug Act that established federal responsibility for inspecting products to protect consumers. In passing the Hepburn Act in 1906 the government was to maintain the control especially on interstate commerce Commission's regulatory powers over the railroads. *[Theodore Roosevelt Biography, Wikipedia, the free encyclopedia]*

CHAPTER 2

Woodrow Wilson is Called the "Godfather of Liberalism"

What is dignity? **Webster** says it is "The quality or state of being **worthy**, honored, or **esteemed**." It is my feeling that entitlements do the opposite. They take dignity away from the individual. That is what the Masters did in the old South to the slaves, and my analogy is that it is what the government of today in Washington DC is doing to the entitlement citizens of today. What occurs then is that individuals do not feel worthy of more than what the government is giving them and the results of that is an inferiority complex that makes them feel that they are not as good as everyone else, and they don't deserve more. The problem is that most of the time they do not realize what is happening to them. They become controlled by the government. There is no self-esteem left to better themselves and they are waiting for the next hand out. How did this come about? It did not happen overnight and did not happen because one President made it happen in a few years. The accumulation through the years from the policies of many Presidents has resulted in programs that were intended to help our citizens that have now been taken advantage of.

You could say it all started with President Wilson, who many believe was the first progressive president. President Wilson, in his first term, persuaded a Democratic Congress

5

to pass major progressive reforms. President Wilson also had Congress pass the Adamson Act, which imposed an 8-hour workday for railroads. Historian John M. Cooper argues that, in his first term, Wilson successfully pushed a legislative agenda that few presidents have equaled which, until President Roosevelt came along who successfully got the Federal Reserve Act passed with his New Deal at which time, along with Wilson's progressive Adamson Act, the country fell into a very progressive state. It might also be mentioned before going back to President Wilson that President Roosevelt got the Federal Reserve Act, the Federal Trade Commission Act, the Clayton Antitrust Act, the Federal Farm Loan Act, and an income tax passed.

President Wilson implemented a policy of racial desegregation for government workers and promised African Americans that he would assist them in advancing their race. President Wilson was considered a liberal but was also well-known as a racist in his policy and politics. He was more concerned with domestic liberalism and being a racist seemed to fit him and he was comfortable with it.

It has become fashionable today for those who once called themselves "liberals" to refer to themselves instead as "progressives." This is a phenomenon evident both among our politicians and among our intellectual class. Citizens who are concerned with the battle of ideas today must therefore endeavor to come to terms both with contemporary progressivism and with its foundational principles from the original turn-of-the-century movement. In order to understand both the Progressive Movement itself and its influence on politics today, there is no more important figure to engage than Woodrow Wilson. There may have been Presidents and politicians before President Wilson to advocate liberalism, but he is known by most as the "Godfather of Liberalism." *[The Heritage Foundation – "Woodrow Wilson: Godfather of Liberalism" July 31, 2012]*

To understand entitlement in the United States, we need to go back to the main social programs in the United States which are welfare subsidies designed to aid the needs of the

U.S. population. These federal programs began with Theodore Roosevelt's **New Nationalism** and expanded with Woodrow Wilson's **New Freedom,** Franklin D. Roosevelt's **New Deal**, John F. Kennedy's **New Frontier**, and Lyndon B. Johnson's **Great Society,** and today has expanded into a complete socialistic society that was being imposed on the American people by Barack Obama. There has not been a name given yet for his programs, except for his trying to get the United States into a complete Socialistic Society where the population is depending on the government as their Master. Let us examine each of these concepts which led us to today's society where the dignity of the individual is being taken away. Remember -- many feel it is the responsibility of the government to provide food, shelter, education and whatever else the needs of the individual may be. It is also believed by many that this is necessary since corporations and private organizations are not providing for the so-called needy. When welfare social programs consist of 35% of the GNP there is something wrong and it will get to the crossroad where the American government - "mostly politicians" - will have a decision to make as to what type of country we want to live in or let our grandchildren inherit. So, what has happened? As time went on with each different president there was a building block. Each one just added more to the welfare system where eventually it was too big for anyone to do anything about it. To do anything would cause a social revolution, so whether Democrat or Republican you had to satisfy the constituents or you didn't get back in office.

Following is a timeline of welfare in the United States taken from *[Wikipedia: Social Programs in the United States].*

1880s–1890s: Attempts were made to move poor people from work yards to poor houses if they were in search of relief funds.

1893–1894: Attempts were made at the first unemployment payments but were unsuccessful due to the 1893–1894 recession.

1932: The Great Depression had gotten worse and the first attempts to fund relief failed. The "Emergency Relief Act", which gave local governments $300 million, was passed into law.

1933: In March 1933, President Franklin D. Roosevelt pushed Congress to establish the **Civilian Conservation Corps** ("CCC"). **CCC** was a public work relief program that operated from 1933 to 1942 in the United States for unemployed, unmarried men from relief families as part of the New Deal. Originally for young men ages 18–23, it was eventually expanded to young men ages 17-28.

1935: The Social Security Act was passed on June 17, 1935. The bill included direct relief (cash, food stamps, etc.) and changes for unemployment insurance.

1940: Aid to Families With Dependent Children (AFDC) was established.

1964: Johnson's War on Poverty is underway, and the Economic Opportunity Act was passed. Commonly known as "the Great Society" **The Economic Opportunity Act of 1964**, authorized the formation of local Community Action Agencies as part of the War on Poverty. These agencies are directly regulated by the federal government. "It is the purpose of The Economic Opportunity Act to strengthen, supplement, and coordinate efforts in furtherance of that policy".

1996: Passed under Clinton, the "Personal Responsibility and Work Opportunity Reconciliation Act of 1996" becomes law. This is a United States federal law considered to be a fundamental shift in both the method and goal of federal cash assistance to the poor. The bill added a workforce development component to welfare legislation, encouraging employment among the poor. The bill was a cornerstone of the Republican Contract with America and was introduced by Rep. E. Clay Shaw, Jr. (R-FL-22). Bill Clinton signed PRWORA into law on August 22, 1996, fulfilling his 1992 campaign promise to "end welfare as we have come to know it".

Additionally, in 2009 we had the passing of the so-called ObamaCare program, or the Affordable Care Act, for health insurance for the millions who supposedly did not have or could not afford health care.

Is free enterprise over or more entitlement coming to an end? Michael Barone, a writer for The Washington Examiner, states that **"History suggests that the era of entitlements is nearly over"**. He writes about how American-sounding intervals of 76 years or life spans of entitlement are just a few years more than the biblical lifespan of three score and ten. *[The following quote was from an Obama-Era presidency and was taken from Michael Barone's Book "The Almanac of American Politics".]*

"It was 76 years from Washington's First Inaugural in 1789 to Lincoln's Second Inaugural in 1865. It was 76 years from the surrender at Appomattox Courthouse in 1865 to the attack at Pearl Harbor in 1941.

Going backward, it was 76 years from the First Inaugural in 1789 to the Treaty of Utrecht in 1713, which settled one of the British-French colonial wars. And going 76 years back from Utrecht takes you to 1637, when the Virginia and Massachusetts Bay colonies were just getting organized.

As for our times, we are now 71 years away from Pearl Harbor. The current 76-year interval ends in December 2017.

Each of these 76-year periods can be depicted as a distinct unit. In the Colonial years up to 1713, very small numbers of colonists established separate cultures that have persisted to our times.

From 1713 to 1789, the colonies were peopled by much larger numbers of motley and often involuntary settlers -- slaves, indentured servants, the unruly Scots-Irish on the Appalachian frontier.

From 1789 to 1865, Americans sought their manifest destiny by expanding across the continent. They made great technological advances but were faced with the irreconcilable issue of slavery in the territories.

The 1865-to-1941 period saw a vast efflorescence of market capitalism, European immigration, and rising standards of living.

The 70-plus years since 1941 have seen a vast increase in the welfare safety net and governance by cooperation among big units -- big government, big business, big labor -- that began in the New Deal and gained steam in and after World War II. I immodestly offer my own "Our Country: The Shaping of America from Roosevelt to Reagan."

The original arrangements in each 76-year period became unworkable and unraveled toward its end. Eighteenth-century Americans rejected the colonial status quo and launched a revolution, then established a constitutional republic.

Nineteenth-century Americans went to war over expansion of slavery. Early-20th-century Americans grappled with the collapse of the private-sector economy in the Depression of the 1930s.

We are seeing something like this again today. The welfare state arrangements that once seemed solid are on the path to unsustainability.

Entitlement programs -- Social Security, Medicare, Medicaid – Obama Care are threatening to gobble up the whole government and much of the private sector, as well.

Lifetime employment by one big company represented by one big union is a thing of the past. People who counted on corporate or public-sector pensions are seeing them default.

Looking back, we are as far away in time today from victory in World War II in 1945 as Americans were at the time of the Dred Scott decision from the First Inaugural.

We are as far away in time today from passage of the Social Security Act in 1935 as Americans then were from the launching of post-Civil War Reconstruction.

Nevertheless, our current president and most politicians of his party seem determined to continue the current welfare state arrangements -- historian Walter Russell Mead calls this the blue-state model -- into the indefinite future.

Some leaders of the other party are advancing ideas for adapting a system that worked reasonably well in an industrial age dominated by seemingly eternal big units into something that can prove workable in an information age experiencing continual change and upheaval wrought by innovations in the market economy. The current 76-year period is nearing its end. What will come next?"

{*Author's Note: This is a very interesting question that indicates, by the trend of events, one of two things must happen:*

a. *The trend continues and we become a socialistic state where free enterprise will not continue to exist, and the working population will be taxed to a point that there will be chaos that will make the Boston Tea Party look like a Sunday brunch; or*
b. *The politicians will wake up in the wake of what has continued to happen with the introduction of Obama Care and the increase in food stamps and start a trend to reverse the entitlement situation in this country.*

One thing is for sure - you cannot afford to take in $2.2 trillion and pay out over $3.2 trillion. Someone has to pay.

Are the American people becoming slaves under the entitlement system being imposed upon them by the socialist _wing of the far-left Democratic Party? I say far left because I do not believe that all Democrats feel that way, although many continue to vote that way so as not to antagonize the party. And most important - does the entitlement population understand what is happening to them? I guess you may ask, "Do they care, or have they just become passive?"}_

CHAPTER 3

Roosevelt's New Deal

Let us start with President Theodore Roosevelt's New Nationalism. Roosevelt made the case for what he called the New Nationalism in a speech in Osawatomie, Kansas, on August 31, 1910. *[Theodore Roosevelt Biography, Wikipedia, the free encyclopedia]* He argued for the protection of human rights and private property rights. He also argued that human welfare was more important than property rights and that only a strong federal government could control the economy and have social justice for the human welfare state. In order to do so, as with Barack Obama, the president needs to make social justice his main priority. Again, as with Barack Obama, Roosevelt wanted executive agencies to regulate the government, not the courts. It was the duty of the federal government to protect the laboring man or the unions. The progressives of the 21st Century advocate today many of Roosevelt's New Deal policies.

Roosevelt's platform called for the following: *[Progressive Party (United States, 1912, the free encyclopedia]*

The platform's main theme was reversing the domination of politics by business interests, which allegedly controlled the Republican and Democratic parties, alike. The platform asserted that:

To destroy this invisible Government, to dissolve the unholy alliance between corrupt business and corrupt politics is the first task of the statesmanship of the day.

13

To that end, the platform called for:

- Strict limits and disclosure requirements on political campaign contributions.
- Registration of lobbyists
- Recording and publication of Congressional committee proceedings.

In the social sphere, the platform called for:

- A National Health Service to include all existing government medical agencies.
- Social insurance, to provide for the elderly, the unemployed, and the disabled.
- Limiting the ability of judges to order injunctions to limit labor strikes
- A minimum wage law for women.
- An eight-hour workday.
- A Federal securities commission
- Farm relief
- Workers' compensation for work-related injuries
- An inheritance tax

The political reforms proposed included:

- Women's suffrage;
- Direct election of Senators; and
- Primary elections for state and federal nominations
- Easier amending of the United States Constitution

The platform also urged states to adopt measures for "direct democracy", including:

- The recall election (citizens may remove an elected official before the end of his term)

- The referendum (citizens may decide on a law by popular vote)
- The initiative (citizens may propose a law by petition and enact it by popular vote)

The book ***The Promise of American Life,*** written in 1909 by Herbert Croly, influenced Theodore Roosevelt. New Nationalism was in direct contrast with Woodrow Wilson's policy of The New Freedom, which promoted antitrust modification, tariff reduction, and banking and currency reform.

National Health Insurance

Needless to say, as President, Theodore Roosevelt did not get everything. For example, National Health Insurance did not come into effect until Barack Obama became President, and that insurance was not really a National Insurance that Obama had hoped for. And then it does not include all the government health insurance companies. Its target is attempting to insure those who could not afford health insurance. As in other government programs, when the government gets involved, it usually gets corrupt or just does not work.

Social insurance did not really happen until Medicare came along In the United States, **Medicare** is a national social insurance program, administered by the U.S. federal government signed into law in 1965 by President Johnson, that guarantees access to health insurance for Americans aged 65 and older and younger people with disabilities as well as people with end stage renal disease. It became a program that was administered by social security. We will talk more about this program under President's Johnson's **Great Society Program** of the 60's. Social Security was set up for retirees when they had reached retirement age whether 62 or 65. But the problem is that when it was initiated, the life expectancy was around 50. Today, life expectancy is approaching 80, so the balance of workers paying in versus the ones drawing has or is coming close to

1:2 (one person paying in for every two collecting benefits). So where will the money continue to come from? President George Bush wanted an investment program where individuals would invest into a private fund for their retirement, but that did not go anywhere. So where does the future of this entitlement go? At the pace it is going now it will soon be broke. As stated in a later chapter, it was used to fund a war which should have never been waged. The government will have to pour money into the program. How do you tell citizens at the time of retirement that they will not receive their social security benefit that they have paid into for their entire working lives?

Limited Injunction in Strikes

As far as Theodore Roosevelt's "limited injunctions in strikes", he was not a wild-eyed unionist who never listened to the business side of things. He opposed labor boycotts, force during strikes (by strikers or anyone else), and unions meddling in politics. On one occasion, Roosevelt sent federal troops to Morenci, Arizona, to break up a mine strike, though he did withdraw when he realized they were only good for intimidating the strikers. He refused to condemn publicly the use of illegal force by the mining corporations in Colorado, although he criticized them privately. Roosevelt was quite sympathetic to the corporations; his support of labor stemmed mostly from a balanced view of the issues. He was quoted saying: "I would guarantee by every means in my power the right of laboring men to join a union, and their right to work as union men without illegal interference from either capitalists or nonunion men". Roosevelt believed in unions in principle; although he did not want either labor forces or capitalists to go too far in asserting their 'rights.' Big labor, like big capital, he remarked, was one of the laws of the social and economic development of the age. He believed that unions contributed to the general welfare and the growth of America.

Minimum Wage and Women's Suffrage

A minimum wage in 1902 was $0.22 per hour and women were paid less than $0.20 per hour. Through Roosevelt's administration the minimum hourly wage went to approximately $0.25 per hour, so there was not much of an increase although in both campaigns Theodore Roosevelt announced he would increase the wages, which he did not do, nor did he do much for equal pay for women. The eight-hour workday started to come into effect primarily because the unions fought for it.

Farm Relief

President Roosevelt favored immediate farm relief and many of the bills he passed in his New Deal, having to do with flood control and helping the farmers, were based on the Progressive Party under Theodore Roosevelt. President Roosevelt stated that the crux of the problem was not the price the farmer got for his products, but rather it assisted in giving him an opportunity to help himself by a system of marketing standardization. He asserted that he would do his utmost to extend the marketing facilities of the farmer so that a government inspector would grade the produce at the points of departure and arrival. Thus, the shipment could be sold at once without bargaining and haggling on the part of the farmer or his representatives. The benefits from such a system would be manifold. It would provide a quick turnover for the farmer and would release his limited capital, which otherwise would remain tied up in the goods. Turning to another phase of the farming problem, Roosevelt pointed out that unnecessary expense both to the farmer and the consumer were involved in the present system of sending produce from country districts to big cities and then back again to smaller towns. Roosevelt proposed to remedy this wasteful condition by an increased marketing reports service through which the farmer could be kept in closer touch with the market. Roosevelt signed the **Newlands Reclamation Bill**, which used money from federal land sales to build reservoirs and irrigation works to promote agriculture in the arid West.

Workers compensation and Work Related Injuries

New Nationalism was Theodore Roosevelt's Progressive political philosophy during the 1912 election and one of his programs that he advocated for was Workers compensation for work-related injuries. Whether this can be classified as an entitlement program could be argued. It is a program that protects all workers and is necessary to protect the workers on highly hazardous jobs such as occurs in construction. It is discussed here because it is also an insurance program advocated by the government, and employees, under the Workers Compensation Act, and many employees who do become disabled on their job can collect under the Social Security Disability Program. This is entitlement, and the remainder of the taxpayers should not be penalized because a company was irresponsible with its employees.

An Inheritance Tax.

President Roosevelt said in 1910, "We grudge no man a fortune in civil life if it is honorably obtained and well used. It is not even enough that it should have been gained without doing damage to the community. We should permit it to be gained only so long as the gaining represents benefit to the community… The really big fortune, the swollen fortune, by the mere fact of its size, acquires qualities which differentiate it in kind as well as in degree from what is possessed by men of relatively small means. Therefore, I believe in a graduated income tax on big fortunes, and … a graduated inheritance tax on big fortunes, properly safeguarded against evasion, and increasing rapidly in amount with the size of the estate." Republicans have fought to get rid of the inheritance tax since 1940 but failed to remember it was members of their own party who created the tax.

18

In 1916, eight years after Theodore Roosevelt left office, Congress finally recognized the justice of his case and incorporated a levy on estates into the tax code.

Income Tax.

Theodore Roosevelt championed the idea that the rich should not only pay more money but at a higher rate, arguing explicitly that it contradicted the spirit of socialism. Roosevelt went on to say, "A heavy progressive tax upon a very large fortune is in no way such a tax upon thrift or industry as a like would be on a small fortune. No advantage comes either to the country as a whole or to the individuals inheriting the money by permitting the transmission in their entirety of the enormous fortunes which would be affected by such a tax; and as an incident to its function of revenue raising, such a tax would help to preserve a measurable equality of opportunity for the people of the generations growing. We have not the slightest sympathy with that socialistic idea which would try to put laziness, shiftlessness and inefficiency on a par with industry. Thrift and efficiency, which would strive to break up not merely private property, but what is far more important, the home, the chief prop upon which our whole civilization stands. Such a theory, if ever adopted, would mean the ruin of the entire country–a ruin which would bear heaviest upon the weakest, upon those least able to shift for themselves. But proposals for legislation such as this herein advocated are directly opposed to this class of socialistic theories. Our aim is to recognize what Lincoln pointed out: The fact that there are some respects in which men are obviously not equal; but also to insist that there should be an equality of self-respect and of mutual respect, an equality of rights before the law, and at least an approximate equality in the conditions under which each man obtains the chance to show the stuff that is in him when compared to his fellows."

"At many stages in the advance of humanity, this conflict between the men who possess more than they have earned and the men who have earned more than they possess is the central condition of progress. In our day it appears as the struggle of freemen to gain and hold the right of self-government as against the special interests, who twist the methods of free government into machinery for defeating the popular will. At every stage, and under all circumstances, the essence of the struggle is to equalize opportunity, destroy privilege, and give to the life and citizenship of every individual the highest possible value both to himself and to the commonwealth. *{End of excerpt from The Promise of American Life by Herbert Croly}*

No man should receive a dollar unless that dollar has been fairly earned. Every dollar received should represent a dollars' worth of service rendered. The really big fortune, the swollen fortune, by the mere fact of its size, acquires qualities which differentiate it in kind as well as in degree from what is possessed by men of relatively small means. Therefore, I believe in a graduated income tax on big fortunes, and in another tax which is far more easily collected and far more effective, a graduated inheritance tax on big fortunes, properly safeguarded against evasion, and increasing rapidly in amount with the size of the estate." [The American Yawp Reader: Theodore Roosevelt on "The New Nationalism" (1910)]

Author's Summary of Theodore Roosevelt

Many would look at Theodore Roosevelt as the one who started The Progressive Movement, not President Wilson. My analysis is that although he had some progressive ideas by some Republican standards, it is the author's opinion that at the turn of the century some things needed changing to help the people. Theodore Roosevelt was the President that came along to initiate these changes that were needed, such as farm relief. Looking at history and the turn of the century at that time manufacturers textile mills etc. were slave shops where owners did basically what they wanted. It was time for a change, so any President who initiated any type of change for the people might be considered a progressive. My analysis is that he was not.

Many Republicans of today might not want to associate themselves with Theodore Roosevelt from this mere fact that they did consider him a Progressive and he should be given credit for starting the progressive movement. You might even go as far to say he was an advocate of income distribution. He believed that since the wealthy made their money form the land or from manufacturing where people worked, that a portion of the income they made should be given back to the government. And where did that money go? The point, is basically, that there is nothing wrong in paying your fair share of taxes, and most don't mind that. They do mind, however, where it might be spent, which in many instances is back to the people in the form of some type of entitlement such as a National Health Service to include all existing government medical social insurance, to provide for the elderly, the unemployed, and the disabled, farm relief, workers compensation for work-related injuries which today is paid for through the social security administration for anyone who winds up becoming disabled on the job.

CHAPTER 4

Woodrow Wilson's New Freedom

President Wilson is considered to be the Father of Progressiveness. One of those who shares that thought is Glen Beck who, when he was on Fox News, commented many times about Wilson's Progressiveness. Let us examine President Wilson even further. When Woodrow Wilson, (a Democrat) won the election of 1912 he received only 42% of the vote. The Progressive candidates - Roosevelt, Taft and Socialist union leader, Eugene Debs votes totaled 58% of the vote. Clearly America still sought progressive change. Wilson, an educator and the son of a Presbyterian Minister, recognized this and embarked on a program to continue Progressive reform called the "**New Freedom**." He enhanced the entitlement movement created by Theodore Roosevelt; but remember -- back then it wasn't considered entitlement.

Shown below are some of the reform movements from Woodrow Wilson's "**New Freedom**" reforms which was taken from the reform bill of Woodrow Wilson in the history of Woodrow Wilson in *Wikipedia* and included the:

1. **Tariff Reform**

    a. Underwood Tariff of 1913
    b. First lowering of tariffs since the Civil War
    c. Went against the protectionist lobby

2.   Business Reform

Wilson's program was known as the **New Freedom**. (The phrase came after the campaign, as the title of a book of his speeches, and as the slogan for his administration's policies.) Wilson believed government's role was to create a level playing field. Then individual energy and business competition would give American lives both decent working conditions, living conditions, and freedom from big-brother intrusions. His solution for monopoly was antitrust prosecution and break-up.

3.   Federal Trade Act (1914)

He set up the FTC or Federal Trade Commission office to investigate and halt unfair and illegal business practices. The FTC could put a halt to these illegal business practices by issuing what is known as a "cease and desist order."

4.   Clayton Antitrust Act (1914)

- Declared certain businesses illegal (interlocking directorates, trusts, horizontal mergers)
- Unions and the Grange were not subject to antitrust laws. This made unions legal!
- Strikes, boycotts, picketing and the collection of strike benefit funds were ruled legal.

5.   Banking Reform

Needed elastic currency, ability to control the amount of money in circulation.

a. Creation of Federal Reserve system.
b. Federal Reserve Banks in 12 districts would print and coin money as well as set interest rates. In this way the "Fed," as it was called, could control the money supply and affect the value of currency. The more money in

23

circulation; the lower the value, and inflation went up. The less money in circulation; the greater the value, and this would lower inflation.

3. Federal Farm Loan Act

Wilson set up the Federal Farm Loan Act for Banks to support farmers. This farm program has expanded today where it is uncontrollable. The government is paying farmers to NOT grow crops and, in some cases, they are being paid to dump the crop. In Northern Maine, when I was growing up, I would see many farmers dump potatoes because there was an abundance. I wonder where the justification for that lies since there are so many folks in the world that are starving. Figure that out.

Like Theodore Roosevelt before him, Woodrow Wilson regarded himself as the personal representative of the people. "No one but the President," he said, "seems to be expected... to look out for the general interests of the country." He developed a program of progressive reform and asserted international leadership in building a new world order. In 1917 he proclaimed America's entrance into World War I a crusade to make the world "safe for democracy." Such as the following, taken from *[Wikipedia's History of Woodrow Wilson:]*

a. Federal Reserve Act, which is an independent agency of the United States government, established in 1914 by the Federal Trade Commission Act. Its principal mission is the promotion of consumer protection and the elimination and prevention of anticompetitive business practices, such as coercive monopoly. The Federal Trade Commission Act was one of President Woodrow Wilson's major acts against trusts. Trusts and trust-busting were significant political concerns during the Progressive Era. The **Federal Reserve Act,** enacted on December 23, 1913, is an Act that created and set up the Federal Reserve System, the central banking system of the United States of America, and granted it the legal authority to issue Federal Reserve Notes (now commonly known as the U.S. Dollar) and Federal Reserve Bank Notes as legal tender. The Act was signed into law by President Woodrow Wilson.

b. The **Clayton Antitrust Act** was enacted on October 15, 1914, to add further substance to the U.S. antitrust law regime by seeking to prevent anticompetitive practices in their incipiency. That regime started with the Sherman Antitrust Act of 1890, the first Federal law outlawing practices considered harmful to consumers (monopolies, cartels, and trusts). The Clayton Act specified particular prohibited conduct, the three-level enforcement scheme, the exemptions, and the remedial measures.

c. The **Federal Farm Loan Act** of 1916 was a United States federal law aimed at increasing credit to rural family farmers. It did so by creating a federal farm loan board, twelve regional farm loan banks and tens of farm loan associations. The act was signed into law by President of the United States, Woodrow Wilson.

d. An income tax which, in the United States, is a tax imposed on income by the federal, most state, and many local, governments. The income tax is determined by applying a tax rate (which may increase as income increases), to taxable income as defined. Individuals and corporations are directly taxable, and estates and trusts may be taxable on undistributed income.

e. And Child labor was curtailed by the Keating–Owen Act of 1916, but the U.S. Supreme Court declared it unconstitutional in 1918.

f. Wilson also had Congress pass the Adamson Act, which imposed an 8-hour workday for railroads.

• *[Wikipedia's History of Woodrow Wilson:]*

Wilson, at first unsympathetic, became a major advocate for women's suffrage after public pressure convinced him that to oppose women's suffrage was politically unwise. Although Wilson promised African Americans "fair dealing...in advancing the interests of their race in the United States", the Wilson administration implemented a policy of racial segregation for federal employees. Although considered a modern liberal visionary giant as President, in terms of implementing domestic race relations, however, Wilson was "deeply racist in his thoughts and politics, and apparently was comfortable being so. Most information here was taken from *["The Life in the White House" by Alda D Donald]*

In October of 1913, President Wilson signed the Revenue Act into law, also known as the **Underwood Tariff**. Tariffs had long been a topic of political interest, and Wilson had written on the subject several times. He had also made his position on tariff reduction part of his campaigning platform in 1912. Wilson was a proponent of Free Trade and low tariffs, and in order to lower tariffs but not lose government revenue, some other means of recouping it were necessary.

The Revenue Act of 1913 also created a new group of tax-exempt organizations dedicated to social welfare in a provision that was a precursor to what is now the Internal Revenue Code section. The Act also provided for the establishment of the income tax to compensate for the loss of revenue due to Wilson's cutting out the tariff on products coming into the country. Wilson knew he had to make up for the loss of revenue that the imports were bringing in for revenue. The Sixteenth Amendment was ratified on February 3, 1913. The Act provided in part that, subject only to such exemptions and deductions as are hereinafter allowed,

a. the gross income of a taxable person shall include gains, profits, and income derived from salaries, wages, or compensation for personal service of whatever kind and in whatever form paid, or from professions, vocations, businesses, trade, commerce, or sales, or dealings in property, whether real or personal, growing out of the ownership or use of or interest in real or personal property,

b. also, from interest, rent, dividends, securities, or the transaction of any lawful business carried on for gain or profit, or gains or profits and income derived from any source whatever. *["What is Income" – from a Truth-Attack article]*

The incomes of couples exceeding $4,000, as well as those of single persons earning $3,000 or more, were subject to a one percent federal tax. Further, the measure provided a progressive tax structure, meaning that high income earners were required to pay at higher rates.

It would require only a few years for the federal income tax to become the chief source of income for the government, far outdistancing tariff revenues. Less than 1% of the population paid federal income tax at the time. In 2013, we had a situation where 3% of the population pays 80% of the taxes and 49% do not pay any taxes. What Wilson started has now blossomed to a situation that 49% of the population are on some type of entitlement that is sponsored by the ones paying the taxes.

Summary of Woodrow Wilson

President Wilson's health and welfare programs continue with him being known, as previously mentioned, as "The Father of Progressiveness" or I might say the Father of Entitlement. His programs include the following which was taken from the *[Fourteen Points – National World War I Museum and Memorial]*

- The Cutter Service Act of 1914 emphasized providing otherwise-unobtainable medical services for men on board American fishing fleets. It authorized the Commandant of the Revenue Cutter Service to *"detail for duty on revenue cutters such surgeons and other persons of the Public Health Service as necessary."*
- The Federal Aid Road Act of 1916, (also known as the Bankhead-Shackleford Act), 39 Stat. 355, was enacted on July 11, 1916, and was the first federal highway funding legislation in the United States.
- The Rural Post "Good" Roads Act of 1916. provided federal aid to the states for the construction of rural post roads. The term "rural post road" was construed to mean any public road over which the United States mail was then transported
- The Sundry Civil Appropriations Act authorized $200,000 for the newly formed Division of Scientific Research for the United States Public Health Service.
- An Act was passed (1916) authorizing hospital and medical services to government employees injured at work.
- An anti-narcotics law was passed (1914), which was the **Harrison Narcotics Tax Act** (Ch. 1, 38 Stat. 785). It was a United States federal law that regulated and taxed the production, importation, and distribution of opiates and Coca products. The act was proposed by

28

Representative Francis Burton Harrison of New York and was approved on December 17, 1914.

- The United State Housing Corporation was established (1918) to build housing projects for wartime workers.
- In 1918, the first Federal grants to States for public health services were made available.
- A federal leprosy hospital was authorized (1917).
- The Civil Service Retirement System was established (1920) to provide pensions to retired civilian federal employees.
- The Civilian Vocational Rehabilitation Act of 1920 (Smith-Fess Act) authorized a joint federal-state vocational rehabilitation program for handicapped civilians.

The Death on the High Seas Act (1920) aimed at compensating the wives of sailors who had lost their lives at sea. The legislation enabled survivors "to recover pecuniary damages, or the lost wages of their relatives on whom they depended upon financially.

CHAPTER 5

Franklin D. Roosevelt's New Deal

Franklin Roosevelt's New Deal was most notable for

a. Ending the Great Depression;
b. Providing moderate social reform without radical revolution or reactionary fascism;
c. Undermining state and local government;
d. Aiding big cities at the expense of farmers, and;
e. Attacking the American capitalist system. *[taken from Quizlet Chapter 33]*

{*Author's Note: We will look at each of these and understand how they also helped spear head and lead into the entitlement society of the 21st Century in the U.S. What is being explained here is that as one President left office, and another took office the entitlements stayed with the incumbent President. No President came in and said we need to get rid of this or that. They probably assumed that the votes would go with the program that was being ended.*}

The Great Depression

I used to hear my father talk about the Great Depression, as a kid, not yet a teenager. When it started; he got a job in the lumber camps in Northern Maine carrying water for the lumberjacks. And then later became a lumberjack himself. I guess that is why in life his feelings for President Franklin Roosevelt were so high. He felt if it wasn't for President Roosevelt America would not have gotten out of the Depression. There was reason at that time to feel that way; the problem is that many of the entitlement programs stayed with us and got built on from there through future Presidents. I know that the harsh years my father had as a young man stayed with him.

Listed here are **five reasons** that many say were the cause of the Great Depression:

1.   Stock Market Crash of 1929

Many believe that the stock market crash that occurred on Black Tuesday, October 29, 1929, is one and the same with the Great Depression. In fact, it was one of the major causes that led to the Great Depression. Two months after the original crash in October, stockholders had lost more than $40 billion dollars.

{Author's Note: Even though the stock market began to regain some of its losses, by the end of 1930, it just was not enough, and America truly entered what is called the Great Depression.}

2.   Bank Failures

Throughout the 1930s, over 9,000 banks failed. Bank deposits were uninsured and thus as banks failed people simply lost their savings. Surviving banks, unsure of the economic situation and concerned for their own survival, stopped being as willing to create new loans.

{Author's Note: This exacerbated the situation leading to less and less expenditures.}

3.   Reduction in Purchasing Across the Board

With the stock market crash and the fears of further economic woes, individuals from all classes stopped purchasing items. This then led to a reduction in the number of items produced and thus a reduction in the workforce. The unemployment rate also rose above 25% which meant even less spending to help alleviate the economic situation.

{*Author's Note: As people lost their jobs, they were unable to keep up with paying for items they had bought through installment plans and their items were repossessed. More and more inventory began to accumulate.*}

4.   American Economic Policy with Europe

As businesses began failing, the government created the Smoot-Hawley Tariff in 1930 to help protect American companies. This charged a high tax for imports thereby leading to less trade between America and foreign countries along with some economic retaliation.

5.   Drought Conditions

While not a direct cause of the Great Depression, the drought that occurred in the Mississippi Valley in 1930 was of such proportions that many could not even pay their taxes or other debts and had to sell their farms for no profit to themselves. *["Causes of the Great Depression – Hackensackschools.org]*
{*Author's Note: The area was nicknamed "The Dust Bowl." This was the topic of John Steinbeck's The Grapes of Wrath.*}

Many farms were left vacant, and farmers moved on to California and other states. This also left the country without a lot of crops producing products that were previously grown in the dust bowl.

President Franklin D. Roosevelt signed the Social Security bill in Washington, D.C., on Aug. 14, 1935. Roosevelt won the presidency in a landslide 1932 victory, in the midst of the Great Depression and promised a "new deal" to solve the crisis. Today's entitlement programs are the legacy of those New Deal policies.

The relative modest beginnings of the New Deal turned out to have been relatively unimportant. What was important were the tendencies that were set in motion. All of those unreconstructed Republican opponents of FDR who talked of "socialism," "the foot in the door," "fascism," and so forth had a substantial point. A new world was being set in motion. The pragmatic case-by-case problem solvers were ignoring a whole set of consequences – the dynamics of interventionism. Expanding entitlements became the way that countless politicians, both Democrat and Republican, were elected and re-elected.

{Author's Note": And from 2009 after President Obama got elected, he is carrying on the legacy of President Roosevelt for a truly total Progressive Society.}

Now we see the unsustainability of the current entitlements built on the New Deal "principle." And then we see a government creating a large new one in the midst of the crisis. We are told that Obamacare will save money. Like all of the other entitlements?

{Author's Note: The money has to come from somewhere and someone has to pay for it, which means usually the taxpayers -- and not necessarily the majority of taxpayers.}

We also see the folly of many of the New Deal institutions like Fannie Mae and later Freddie Mac. We see their role in the housing bubble.

{Author's Note: The government kept pouring billions into these programs and they continued to get worse and these agencies kept saying that they are losing money. Money is never made in an entitlement program. The politics of running these programs or agencies cost more than the money that is put into them.}

Now we see the folly of monetary and fiscal policies based on temporary expedients. Economic agents cannot rationally plan when the role of the state is so uncertain and so liable to come up with arbitrary policy interventions, as in the recent bailouts. In many ways, the government told us that the ordinary laws of economics and classical wisdom about sound policy have been temporarily – but indefinitely – suspended.

{Author's Note: As we know, any programs the government institutes never go away.}

Of course, the consequences both for policy and the future of economics depend on the *interpretation* of the financial crisis and the Great Recession. What caused them? What policies are conducive – or at least do not inhibit – recovery. (My late colleague Ludwig Lachmann used to say, "People no doubt learn from experience, but what do they learn?") *[By Mario Rizzo Guest blogger, September 20, 2010, ThinkMarkets.]*

{*Author's Note: It does not seem like anything was learned from the so called "Great Depression." We continue to have recessions and downturns, and the blame goes on and on. It seems that the entitlement government thinks that they can "keep spending and that the money will come."*}

The New Deal did not end the Depression. Even with all the new programs, the government still wasn't spending enough money to jumpstart a stalled economy. Then, in the 1940s, World War II changed the situation. To fight in that war, the government had to purchase guns, tanks, ships, airplanes, and other military equipment. The defense industry hired many people, who then had more money to spend. The U.S. economy started growing again. Although the New Deal didn't end the Depression, it forever changed the U.S. government. As Supreme Court Justice John Clarke told FDR, "You have put a new face upon the social and political life of our country." *[Google.com – "FDR's Response to the Great Depression – Overview of a New Dea]*

President Roosevelt also increased the president's power. Under FDR, the White House became the center of government. More than other early-20th-century residents, Roosevelt proposed entitlement bills and programs for Congress to consider instead of waiting for Congress to act. Other nations also saw the rise of strong leaders, but at the same time, those nations saw a loss of freedom. For example, during the Great Depression, Germany elected Adolf Hitler, who became a dictator. FDR's leadership, and his concern for the poor, helped Americans keep their faith in democracy although it was a democracy that got the population to rely more on the government. As stated, Roosevelt increased the president's power, and Roosevelt also expanded the federal government. Because of the New Deal, the federal government became directly responsible for people's well-being in a way it had not been before. It now made relief payments, served school lunches, and ran a program providing pensions. People came to see the federal government, not their state or local governments, as the protector of their welfare. In a sense you might say the American entrepreneurship started to dwindle. When this occurs, people start to look totally to the government for their survival and lose their self-respect. It becomes "what can big brother do for me?" When this type of entitlement society evolves, the government looks for the rich to support it with excess taxes on anything they can come up with.

The federal government went into debt to provide this aid. The government goes into debt when it spends more than it takes in. Today the answer seems to be to borrow money from other countries, such as China, to whom we owe trillions. Franklin Roosevelt used deficit spending both to fund the New Deal and to pay for the war. Since then, deficit spending has been a consistent part of the federal budget to balance it.

This is not to say that all programs that President Roosevelt proposed and passed were bad. There are certain things the government should be responsible for. Several of FDR's New Deal programs continue to help Americans today. Some of the more important programs that still exist offer the following benefits and protections, some of which were not entirely bad:

1. **<u>Federal Deposit Insurance Corporation</u>**.

Between 1930 and 1933, nearly 9,000 U.S. banks collapsed. American depositors lost $1.3 billion dollars in savings.2 This wasn't the first time Americans had lost their savings during economic downturns, and bank failures occurred repeatedly in the 19th century. President Roosevelt saw an opportunity to end the uncertainty in the American banking system, so depositors wouldn't suffer such catastrophic losses in the future.

The Banking Act of 1933, also known as the Glass-Steagall Act, separated commercial banking from investment banking and regulated them differently. The legislation also established the Federal Deposit Insurance Corporation (FDIC) as an independent agency. The FDIC improved consumer confidence in the banking system by insuring deposits in Federal Reserve member banks, a guarantee they still provide bank customers today. In 1934, only nine of the FDIC-insured banks failed, and no depositors in those failed banks lost their savings.

FDIC insurance was originally limited to deposits up to $2,500. Today, deposits up to $250,000 are protected by the FDIC coverage. Banks pay the insurance premiums to guarantee their customers' deposits.

2.   Federal National Mortgage Association (Fannie Mae).

Much like in the recent financial crisis, the 1930's economic downturn came on the heels of a housing market bubble that burst. By the start of the Roosevelt administration in 1932, nearly half of all American mortgages were in default, and at its worst in 1933, some 1,000 home loans were foreclosed every day. Building construction came to a halt, putting workers out of their jobs and amplifying the economic fallout. As banks failed by the thousands, even worthy borrowers couldn't get loans to buy homes.

The Federal National Mortgage Association, also known as Fannie Mae, was established in 1938 when President Roosevelt signed an amendment to the National Housing Act (passed in 1934). Fannie Mae's purpose was to purchase loans from private lenders, freeing up capital so those lenders could fund new loans. Fannie Mae helped fuel the post-WWII housing boom by financing loans for millions of GIs. Today, Fannie Mae and a companion program, Freddie Mac, are publicly held companies that finance millions of home purchases.

3.   National Labor Relations Board.

Workers at the turn of the 20th century were gaining steam in their efforts to improve working conditions. By the close of World War I, labor unions claimed 5 million members. But management started cracking the whip in the 1920s, using injunctions and restraining orders to stop workers from striking and organizing. Union membership dropped to 3 million, just 300,000 more than pre-WWI numbers.

In February 1935, Sen. Robert F. Wagner of New York introduced the National Labor Relations Act, which would create a new agency dedicated to enforcing employee rights. The National Labor Relations Board was launched when FDR signed the Wagner Act in July of that year. Though the law was initially challenged by business, the U.S. Supreme Court ruled the NLRB was constitutional in 1937.

4.   Securities and Exchange Commission.

After World War I, there was an investment boom in the largely unregulated securities markets. An estimated 20 million investors bet their money on securities, looking to get rich and get their piece of what became a $50 billion pie. When the market crashed in October 1929, those investors lost not only their money but also their confidence in the market.

The main goal of the Securities Exchange Act of 1934 was to restore consumer confidence in the securities markets. The law established the Securities and Exchange Commission to regulate and oversee brokerage firms, stock exchanges, and other agents. FDR appointed Joseph P. Kennedy, father of future President John F. Kennedy, as the SEC's first chairman.

The SEC is still in place, and works to ensure that "all investors, whether large institutions or private individuals...have access to certain basic facts about an investment prior to buying it, and so long as they hold it."

5.   Social Security

In 1930, 6.6 million Americans were age 65 and older. Retirement was nearly synonymous with poverty. As the Great Depression took hold and unemployment rates soared, President Roosevelt and his allies in Congress recognized the need to establish some kind of safety net program for the elderly and disabled. On August 14, 1935, FDR signed the Social Security Act, creating what has been described as the most effective poverty mitigation program in U.S. history.

With the passage of the Social Security Act, the U.S. government established an agency to register citizens for benefits, to collect taxes on both employers and employees to fund the benefits, and to distribute those funds to beneficiaries. Social Security helped not only the elderly, but also the blind, the unemployed, and dependent children.

Social Security provides benefits to over 63 million Americans today, including over 46 million senior citizens. Although some factions in Congress have attempted to privatize or dismantle Social Security in recent years, it remains one of the most popular and effective New Deal programs.

6.   Soil Conservation Service

The U.S. was already in the grip of the Great Depression when things took a turn for the worse. A persistent drought that started in 1932 wreaked havoc on the Great Plains. A massive dust storm, dubbed the Dust Bowl, carried the region's soil away with the wind in the mid-1930s. The problem was literally carried to the steps of Congress, as soil particles coated Washington, D.C., in 1934.

On April 27, 1935, FDR signed legislation establishing the Soil Conservation Service (SCS) as a program of the U.S. Department of Agriculture (USDA). The agency's mission was to study and solve the problem of the nation's eroding soil. The SCS performed surveys and developed flood control plans to prevent soil from being washed away. They also established regional nurseries to cultivate and distribute seeds and plants for soil conservation work.

In 1937, the program was expanded when the USDA drafted the Standard State Soil Conservation Districts Law. Over time, over three thousand Soil Conservation Districts were established to help farmers develop plans and practices for conserving the soil on their land.

During the Clinton administration in 1994, Congress reorganized the USDA and renamed the Soil Conservation Service to reflect its broader scope. Today, the Natural Resources Conservation Service (NRCS) maintains field offices across the country, with staff trained to help landowners implement science-based conservation practices.

7. Tennessee Valley Authority

The Tennessee Valley Authority may be the most surprising success story of the New Deal. Established on May 18, 1933, by the Tennessee Valley Authority Act, the TVA was given a tough but important mission. Residents of the impoverished, rural region desperately needed an economic boost. Private power companies had largely ignored this part of the country, as little profit could be gained by connecting poor farmers to the power grid.

The TVA was tasked with several projects focused on the river basin, which spanned seven states. In addition to producing hydroelectric power for the under-served region, the TVA built dams for flood control, developed fertilizers for agriculture, restored forests and wildlife habitat, and educated farmers about erosion control and other practices to improve food production. In its first decade, the TVA was supported by the Civilian Conservation Corps, which established almost 200 camps in the area.

While many New Deal programs faded when the U.S. entered World War II, the Tennessee Valley Authority played an important role in the country's military success. The TVA's nitrate plants produced the raw materials for munitions. Their mapping department produced the aerial maps used by aviators during campaigns in Europe. And when the U.S. government decided to develop the first atomic bombs, they built their secret city in Tennessee, where they could access millions of kilowatts produced by the TVA.

The Tennessee Valley Authority still provides power to 10 million people in seven states and oversees a combination of hydroelectric, coal-fired, and nuclear power plants. It remains a testament to the enduring legacy of FDR's New Deal. *[ThoughtCo – 7 New Deal Programs Still in Effect Today]*

Author's Summary of Franklin Roosevelt

Despite these lingering disagreements, some New Deal programs are still so popular that everyone supports them. For example, neither party wants to end Social Security, even though the system is in trouble. The truth is the system would not be in trouble if:

a. Only people who actually paid into it got the money;
b. You can only draw from it if you are at retirement age;
c. It is not used as an entitlement program for anyone who needs money to live.

The thinking that suggests that people pay in through payroll taxes today do not completely pay for pensions is not totally true and it would not be so at all if President G. W. Bush could have passed the system where individuals could self-invest through an individual program. This would be a mandatory investment but would be a program that the government would not be able to dip into, as they have done and continue to do with Social Security.

The Social Security system may run out of money sometime in the future. In early 1999, President Bill Clinton announced a plan to save Social Security by using extra money from the federal budget. The Republicans accepted his plan. They knew that saving Social Security is a priority for Americans and that voters might grow angry if they made a political fight of the issue. FDR probably would have approved. "The great public," Roosevelt said, "is interested more in government than in politics." Roosevelt felt that party labels mattered little as long as politicians "did the big job that their times demanded to be done."

CHAPTER 6

John F Kennedy's New Frontier

The term **New Frontier** was used by liberal Democratic presidential candidate John F. Kennedy in his acceptance speech in the 1960 United States presidential election to the Democratic National Convention at the Los Angeles Memorial Coliseum as the Democratic slogan to inspire America to support him. The phrase developed into a label for his administration's domestic and foreign programs. Some say he would be a good Republican today. If that is true, then it goes to show how some people feel the Republican Party has shifted to the left. If that is so thank God, the Tea Party has come into being. Maybe it was needed at this time in history (2013) to wake up the Republican Party. *[Quizlet.com – Chapter 30]*

President Kennedy went on to say: *[taken from the Convention Minutes of the Convention on Google.]*
[W]e stand today on the edge of a New Frontier -— the frontier of the 1960s, the frontier of unknown opportunities and perils, the frontier of unfilled hopes and unfilled dreams.... Beyond that frontier are uncharted areas of science and space, unsolved problems of peace and war, unconquered problems of ignorance and prejudice, unanswered questions of poverty and surplus.

In the words of Robert D. Marcus: "Kennedy entered office with ambitions to eradicate poverty and to raise America's eyes to the stars through the space program". *{Wikipedia: New*

Frontier}. But he did cut taxes and what he was planning on cutting to get his program going after a tax cut is not known. What was coming next for this President was far worse than we could ever imagine, but we will get into that in the next chapter.

After the Eisenhower Administration there was a slight turndown, which is not unusual for some reason it seems that after each administration there is a turndown. The Kennedy Administration needed to push an economic program through congress in an effort to turn around the turndown that was occurring with the American economy. On February 2, 1961, Kennedy sent an economic proposal to Congress that he felt would turn the economy around, which he must have had in the works even during the election. The legislative proposals put forward in this message included:

1. Extending unemployment for an additional thirteen-weeks as a temporary supplement to jobless benefits.
2. The extension of aid to the children of unemployed workers.
3. The redevelopment of distressed areas, which President Johnson attempted to carry out;
4. An increase in Social Security payments and the encouragement of earlier retirement.
5. An increase in the minimum wage.
6. The provision of emergency relief to feed grain farmers.
7. The financing of a comprehensive homebuilding and slum clearance program.

President Kennedy wasted no time because in the next few following months these seven measures became law. Another six measure were signed by the end of June. The economic stimulus program provided an estimated 420,000 construction jobs under a new Housing Act, $175 million in higher wages for those below the new minimum, over $400 million in aid to over 1,000 distressed counties, over $200 million in extra welfare payments to 750,000 children and their parents, and nearly $800 million in extended unemployment benefits for nearly three million unemployed Americans.

In his short time as President, Kennedy went on under his Presidential Authority to also:

- Kennedy carried out various measures to boost the economy under his own executive anti-recessionary acceleration program. Through his own initiative, he directed all Federal agencies to accelerate their procurement and construction, particularly in labor surplus areas. A long-range program of post office construction was compressed into the first six months of his presidency, farm price supports were raised and their payments advanced, over a billion dollars in state highway aid funds were released ahead of schedule, and the distribution of tax refunds and GI life insurance dividends were sped up. In addition, free food distribution to needy families was expanded, state governors were urged by Kennedy to spend federal funds more rapidly for hospitals, schools, roads, and waste treatment facilities, the college housing and urban renewal programs were pushed forward, and procurement agencies were directed to make purchases in areas of high unemployment.
- In an attempt to expand credit and stimulate building, Kennedy ordered a reduction in the maximum permissible interest rate on FHA insured loans, reduced the interest rate on Small Business Administration loans in distressed areas, expanded its available credit and liberalized lending by the Federal Home Loan Banks. The Federal Reserve Board was also encouraged to help keep long-term interest rates low through the purchase of long-term government issues.
- By 1964 economic recovery had begun, as low interest rates in mid-1962 stimulated a boom in the housing

industry, while accelerated expenditures on veterans' benefits, highway building, and other government procurement programs revived consumer demand.

- The Trade Expansion Act of 1962 authorized the President to negotiate tariff reductions on a reciprocal basis of up to 50 percent with the European Common Market. It provided legislative authority for U.S. participation in multilateral trade negotiations from 1964–1967, which became known as the Kennedy Round. The authority expired June 30, 1967, predetermining the concluding date of the Kennedy Round. U.S. duties below five percent *ad valorem*, duties on certain agricultural commodities, and duties on tropical products exported by developing countries could be reduced to zero under the act. The 1962 legislation explicitly eliminated the "Peril Point" provision that had limited U.S. negotiating positions in earlier General Agreement on Tariffs and Trade (GATT) rounds, and instead called on the Tariff Commission and other agencies of the U.S. government to provide the president and his negotiators with information regarding the probable economic effects of specific tariff concessions.

President Kennedy's New Frontier affected all phases of government and individuals on the street. Areas affected were:

a. Taxation
b. Labor
c. Education
d. Welfare
e. Civil rights
f. Housing
g. Unemployment
h. Health
i. Equal rights for women

j. Environment
k. Agriculture
l. Crime
m. Defense

[Taken from Kennedy's Presidential Library and Museum]

As shown, his policies left nothing untouched. Let us look at each of these: *[from which the main source of information is Wikipedia – New Frontier]*

American Economic Policy with Europe

As businesses began failing, the government created the Smoot-Hawley Tariff in 1930 to help protect American companies. This charged a high tax for imports thereby leading to less trade between America and foreign countries along with some economic retaliation.

Economy

The Kennedy Administration pushed an economic stimulus program through congress in an effort to kick-start the American economy following an economic downturn. On February 2, 1961, Kennedy sent a comprehensive Economic Message to Congress which had been in preparation for several weeks. The legislative proposals put forward in this message included:

1. The addition of a temporary thirteen-week supplement to jobless benefits,
2. The extension of aid to the children of unemployed workers,
3. The redevelopment of distressed areas,
4. An increase in Social Security payments and the encouragement of earlier retirement,

5. An increase in the minimum wage and an extension in coverage,

6. The provision of emergency relief to feed grain farmers, and

7. The financing of a comprehensive home building and slum clearance program.

The following month, the first of these seven measures became law, and the remaining six measures had been signed by the end of June. Altogether, the economic stimulus program provided an estimated 420,000 construction jobs under a new Housing Act, $175 million in higher wages for those below the new minimum, over $400 million in aid to over 1,000 distressed counties, over $200 million in extra welfare payments to 750,000 children and their parents, and nearly $800 million in extended unemployment benefits for nearly three million unemployed Americans.

- Under his own presidential authority, Kennedy carried out various measures to boost the economy under his own executive anti-recessionary acceleration program. Through his own initiative, he directed all Federal agencies to accelerate their procurement and construction, particularly in labor surplus areas. A long-range program of post office construction was compressed into the first six months of his presidency, farm price supports were raised and their payments advanced, over a billion dollars in state highway aid funds were released ahead of schedule, and the distribution of tax refunds and GI life insurance dividends were sped up. In addition, free food distribution to needy families was expanded, state governors were urged by Kennedy to spend federal funds more rapidly for hospitals, schools, roads, and waste treatment facilities, the college housing and urban renewal programs were pushed forward, and procurement agencies were directed to make purchases in areas of high unemployment.

- In an attempt to expand credit and stimulate building, Kennedy ordered a reduction in the maximum permissible interest rate on FHA insured loans, reduced the interest rate on Small Business Administration loans in distressed areas, expanded its available credit and liberalized lending by the Federal Home Loan Banks. The Federal Reserve Board was also encouraged to help keep long-term interest rates low through the purchase of long-term government issues.

- By 1964 economic recovery had begun, as low interest rates in mid-1962 stimulated a boom in the housing industry, while accelerated expenditures on veterans' benefits, highway building, and other government procurement programs revived consumer demand.

- The Trade Expansion Act of 1962 authorized the president to negotiate tariff reductions on a reciprocal basis of up to 50 percent with the European Common Market. It provided legislative authority for U.S. participation in multilateral trade negotiations from 1964 to 1967, which became known as the Kennedy Round. The authority expired June 30, 1967, predetermining the concluding date of the Kennedy Round. U.S. duties below five percent *ad valorem*, duties on certain agricultural commodities, and duties on tropical products exported by developing countries could be reduced to zero under the act. The 1962 legislation explicitly eliminated the "Peril Point" provision that had limited U.S. negotiating positions in earlier General Agreement on Tariffs and Trade (GATT) rounds, and instead called on the Tariff Commission and other agencies of the U.S. government to provide the president and his negotiators with information regarding the probable economic effects of specific tariff concessions.

Taxation

Under the Kennedy Administration, the most significant tax reforms since the New Deal were carried out, including a new investment tax credit. President Kennedy said one of the best ways to bolster the economy was to cut taxes, and December 14, 1962, Kennedy stated at the Economic Club of New York that:

The final and best means of strengthening demand among consumers and business is to reduce the burden on private income and the deterrents to private initiative which are imposed by our present tax system; and this administration pledged itself last summer to an across-the-board, top-to-bottom cut in personal and corporate income taxes to be enacted and become effective in 1963. I am not talking about a 'quickie' or a temporary tax cut, which would be more appropriate if a recession were imminent. Nor am I talking about giving the economy a mere shot in the arm, to ease some temporary complaint. I am talking about the accumulated evidence of the last 5 years that our present tax system, developed as it was, in good part, during World War II to restrain growth, exerts too heavy a drag on growth in peace time; that it siphons out of the private economy too large a share of personal and business purchasing power; that it reduces the financial incentives for personal effort, investment, and risk-taking.

Kennedy specifically advocated cutting the corporate tax rate in this same speech. "Corporate tax rates must also be cut to increase incentives and the availability of investment capital. The Government has already taken major steps this year to reduce business tax liability and to stimulate the modernization, replacement, and expansion of our productive plant and equipment. We have done this through the 1962 investment tax credit and through the liberalization of depreciation allowances— two essential parts of our first step in tax revision which amounted to a 10 percent reduction in corporate income taxes worth $2.5 billion." President Kennedy went on to say he favored tax cuts for the rich as well as the poor:

Next year's tax bill should reduce personal as well as corporate income taxes, for those in the lower brackets, who are certain to spend their additional take-home pay, and for those in the middle and upper brackets, who can thereby be encouraged to undertake additional efforts and enabled to invest more capital.

On the same evening, President Kennedy said the private sector and not the public sector was the key to economic growth:

"In short, to increase demand and lift the economy, the Federal Government's most useful role is not to rush into a program of excessive increases in public expenditures, but to expand the incentives and opportunities for private expenditures." President Kennedy told the economic club the impact he expected from tax cuts. "Profit margins will be improved and both the incentive to invest and the supply of internal funds for investment will be increased. There will be new interest in taking risks, in increasing productivity, in creating new jobs and new products for long-term economic growth."

Labor

- Amendments to the Fair Labor Standards Act in 1961 greatly expanded the FLSA's scope in the retail trade sector and increased the minimum wage for previously covered workers to $1.15 an hour effective September 1961 and to $1.25 an hour in September 1963. The minimum for workers newly subject to the Act was set at $1.00 an hour effective September 1961, $1.15 an hour in September 1964, and $1.25 an hour in September 1965. Retail and service establishments were allowed to employ full-time students at wages of no more than 15 percent below the minimum with proper certification from the Department of Labor.

The amendments extended coverage to employees of retail trade enterprises with sales exceeding $1 million annually, although individual establishments within those covered enterprises were exempt if their annual sales fell below $250,000. The concept of enterprise coverage was introduced by the 1961 amendments. Those amendments extended coverage in the retail trade industry from an established 250,000 workers to 2.2 million.

- An Executive Order was issued (1962) which provided federal employees with collective bargaining rights.
- The Federal Salary Reform Act (1962) established the principle of "maintaining federal white-collar wages at a level with those paid to employees performing similar jobs in private enterprises."
- A Postal Service and Federal Employees Salary Act was passed (1962) to reform Federal white-collar statutory salary systems, adjust postal rates, and establish a standard for adjusting annuities under the Civil Service Retirement Act. This legislation marked the first time that a consistent guideline for regular increases was applied to the national pay scales for federal white-collar and postal employees.
- The Contract Work Hours and Safety Standards Act (1962) established "standards for hours, overtime compensation, and safety for employees working on federal and federally funded contracts and subcontracts".
- An 11-member Missile Site Labor Commission was established "to develop procedures for settling disputes on the government's 22 missile bases."
- A pilot program was launched to train and place youths in jobs.
- Paid overtime was granted to workers on government financed construction jobs for work in excess of 40 hours.

Education

- Scholarships and student loans were broadened under existing laws by Kennedy, and new means of specialized aid to education were invented or expanded by the president, including an increase in funds for libraries and school lunches, the provision of funds to teach the deaf, children with physical or cognitive disabilities, and gifted children, the authorization of literacy training under Manpower Development, the allocation of president funds to stop dropouts, a quadrupling of vocational education, and working together with schools on delinquency. Altogether, these measures attacked serious educational problems and freed up local funds for use on general construction and salaries.
- Various measures were introduced which aided educational television, college dormitories, medical education, and community libraries.
- The Educational Television Facilities Act (1962) provided federal grants for new station construction, enabling in-class-room instructional television to operate in thousands of elementary schools, offering primarily religious instruction, music, and arts.
- The Health Professions Educational Assistance Act (1963) provided $175 million over a three-year period for matching grants for the construction of facilities for teaching physicians, dentists, nurses, podiatrists, optometrists, pharmacists, and other health professionals. The Act also created a loan program of up to $2000 per annum for students of optometry, dentistry, and medicine.
- The Vocational Education Act (1963) significantly increased enrollment in vocational education.
- A law was enacted (1961) to encourage and facilitate the training of teachers of the deaf.

- The Fulbright-Hays Act of 1961 enlarged the scope of the Fulbright program while extending it geographically.
- An estimated one-third of all major New Frontier programs made some form of education a vital element, and the Office of Education called it "the most significant legislative period in its hundred-year history".
- The McIntire–Stennis Act of 1962 provided federal financial support to universities and colleges for forestry research and graduate education.

{*Author's Note: My thoughts on this are that you would have thought that with all this money put into education by President Kennedy the U.S. would have, today, the best education system in the world. Although our colleges and universities are still attracting a lot of foreign students, the elementary school system where all the money is going has not done a lot to improve education. My last knowledge is that we were way behind other countries -- approx. 26th in the world in Math and Science. Putting money into something thinking it will fix it is a liberal entitlement idea - what government program has worked under the concept of throwing more money into it and thinking it will solve all the problems?*}

Welfare

- Unemployment and welfare benefits were expanded.
- In 1961, Social Security benefits were increased by 20% and provision for early retirement was introduced, enabling workers to retire at the age of sixty-two while receiving partial benefits. {*Author's Note: Although the elders deserve more since I don't feel we do a great job in caring for our elders, I believe since this time the age*

now for retirement under Social Security has risen to a minimum of 66 years of age.}

- The Social Security Amendments of 1961 permitted male workers to elect early retirement age 62, increased minimum benefits, liberalized the benefit payments to aged widow, widower, or surviving dependent parent, and also liberalized eligibility requirements and the retirement test.

{Author's Note: We know that has since changed.}

- The 1962 amendments to the Social Security Act authorized the federal government to reimburse states for the provision of social services.

{Author's Note: And where do the states get the money?}

- The School Lunch Act was amended for authority to begin providing free meals in poverty-stricken areas.

{Author's Notre: I believe this is where the government does well; to look after the welfare of our children.}

- A pilot food stamp program was launched (1961), covering six areas in the United States. In 1962, the program was extended to eighteen areas, feeding 240,000 people. *{Author's Note: Today there are approx. 49 million on food stamps. It has gotten out of control.}*
- Various school lunch and school milk programs were extended, "enabling 700,000 more children to enjoy a hot school lunch and eighty-five thousand more schools, childcare centers, and camps to receive fresh milk".
- ADC was extended to whole families (1961).
- Aid to Families with Dependent Children (AFDC) replaced the Aid to Dependent Children (ADC)

program, as coverage was extended to adults caring for dependent children.

- A major revision of the public welfare laws was carried out, with a $300 million modernization which emphasized rehabilitation instead of relief"
- A temporary antirecession supplement to unemployment compensation was introduced.
- Food distribution to needy Americans was increased. In January 1961, the first executive order issued by Kennedy mandated that the Department of Agriculture increase the quantity and variety of foods donated for needy households. This executive order represented a shift in the Commodity Distribution Programs' primary purpose, from surplus disposal to that of providing nutritious foods to low-income households.
- Social Security benefits were extended to an additional five million Americans.
- The Self-Employed Individuals Tax Retirement Act (1962) provided self-employed people with a tax postponement for income set aside in qualified pension plans.
- The Public Welfare Amendments of 1962 provided for greater Federal sharing in the cost of rehabilitative services to applicants, recipients, and persons likely to become applicants for public assistance. It increased the Federal share in the cost of public assistance payments and permitted the States to combine the various categories into one category. The amendments also made permanent the 1961 amendment which extended aid to dependent children to cover children removed from unsuitable homes.

{Author's Note: This is an example of the state involving themselves in the private sector and taking away the responsibility of the family. It has grown worse through the years where today the state or Federal government is gaining control of the families.}

- Federal funds were made available for the payment of foster care costs for AFDC-eligible children who had come into state custody.
- An act was approved (1963) which extended for one year the period during which responsibility for the placement and foster care of dependent children, under the program of aid to families with dependent children under Title IV of the Social Security Act.
- Federal civil service retirement benefits were index-linked to changes in the Consumer Price Index (1962).

Civil Rights

- Various measures were carried out by the Kennedy Justice Department to enforce court orders and existing legislation. The Kennedy Administration promoted a Voter Education Project which led to 688,800 between the 1st of April 1962 and the 1st of November 1964, while the Civil Rights Division brought over forty-two suits in four states in order to secure voting rights for black people. In addition, Kennedy supported the anti-poll tax amendment, which cleared Congress in September 1962 (although it was not ratified until 1964 as the Twenty-fourth Amendment). As noted by one student of Black voting in the South, in relation to the attempts by the Kennedy Administration to promote civil rights, "Whereas the Eisenhower lawyers had moved deliberately, the Kennedy-Johnson attorneys pushed the judiciary far more earnestly."
- Executive Order 10925 (issued in 1961) combined the federal employment and government contractor agencies into a unified Committee on Equal Employment opportunity (CEEO). This new committee helped to put an end to segregation and discriminatory employment practices (such as only employing African-Americans

for low-skilled jobs) in a number of workplaces across the United States.

- Executive Order 11063 banned discrimination in federally funded housing.
- The Interstate Commerce Commission made Jim Crow illegal in interstate transportation, having been put under pressure to do so by both the Freedom Riders and the Department of Justice.
- Employment of African-Americans in federal jobs such as in the Post office, the Navy, and the Veterans Administration as a result of the Kennedy Administration's affirmative action policies.
- The Kennedy Administration forbade government contractors from discriminating against any applicant or employee for employment on the grounds of national origin, color, creed, or race.
- The Plan for Progress was launched by the CEEO to persuade large employers to adopt equal opportunity practices. By 1964 268 firms with 8 million employees had signed on to this, while a nationwide study covering the period from May 1961 to June 1963 of 103 corporations "showed a Negro gain from 28,940 to 42,738 salaried and from 171,021 to 198,161 hourly paid jobs".

{Author's Note: President Kennedy probably did more for getting Blacks to vote Democrat than any other President in history. They probably have forgotten that it was a Republican that freed them, and the Democrats were not for it.}

Housing

- The most comprehensive housing and urban renewal program in American history up until that point was carried out, including the first major provisions for middle-income housing, protection of urban open spaces, public mass transit, and private low-income housing.

- Omnibus Housing Bill 1961. In March 1961 President Kennedy sent Congress a special message, proposing an ambitious and complex housing program to spur the economy, revitalize cities, and provide affordable housing for middle- and low-income families. The bill proposed spending $3.19 billion and placed major emphasis on improving the existing housing supply, instead of on new housing starts, and creating a cabinet-level Department of Housing and Urban Affairs to oversee the programs. The bill also promised to make the Federal Housing Administration a full partner in urban renewal program by authorizing mortgage loans to finance rehabilitation of homes and urban renewal Committee on housing combined programs for housing, mass transportation, and open space land bills into a single bill.
- Urban renewal grants were increased from $2 to $4 million, while an additional 100,000 units of public housing were constructed.

{Author's Note: Many of these housing projects that were built are not in existence today. I personally have seen one in New Britain, CT that was turned into a slum and was torn down. It goes to show that when you give someone something and they don't have to pay for it and have not earned it, they will not respect it or take care of it. This is what entitlement does.}

- Opportunities were provided for coordinated planning of community development: technical assistance to state and local governments.
- Under the Kennedy Administration, there was a change of focus from a wrecker ball approach to small rehabilitation projects in order to preserve existing 'urban textures'.
- Funds for housing for the elderly were increased.
- Title V of the Housing Act was amended (1961) to make nonfarm rural residents eligible for direct housing

loans from the Farmers Home Administration. These changes extended the housing program to towns with a population of up to 2,500.

- The Senior Citizens Housing Act (1962) established loans for low-rent apartment projects which were "designed to meet the needs of people aged 62 and over".

{Author's Note: This is one area where the government still does not do enough for the elderly. Especially when they determine that a senior citizen who is getting Social Security is included in the entitlement programs stats. Paying into something your whole life is not entitlement.}

Unemployment

- To help the unemployed, Kennedy broadened the distribution of surplus food, created a "pilot" Food Stamp program for poor Americans, directed that preference be given to distressed areas in defense contracts, and expanded the services of U.S. Employment Offices.

{Author's Note: The Food Stamp Program has been blown out of proportion by President Obama to where approx. 49 million Americans get them. No one wants to deny someone who needs help, but the entitlement of 2013 was abused, and our present entitlement President encourages it and wants it that way. President Obama wanted a Nannie state.}

- Social security benefits were extended to each child whose father was unemployed.

{Author's Note: This encourages entitlement and for parents not to work, since they will now get a larger check from the government for having kids.}

- The first accelerated public works program for areas of unemployment since the New Deal was launched.
- The first full-scale modernization and expansion of the vocational education laws since 1946 were carried out.
- Federal grants were provided to the states enabling them to extend the period covered by unemployment benefit.

{Author's Note: At the end of it all "Federal Government provides to the states." Who pays for this but the poor citizens who are out there working and have their taxes increased. This extension of unemployment encourages people not to go back to work. President Obama had it extended up to 98 weeks. This is not encouragement to return to work.}

- The Manpower Development and Training Act of 1962 authorized a three-year program aimed at retraining workers displaced by new technology. The bill did not exclude employed workers from benefiting and it authorized a training allowance for unemployed participants. Even though 200,000 people were recruited, there was minimal impact, comparatively. The Area Redevelopment Act, a $394 million spending package passed in 1961, followed a strategy of investing in the private sector to stimulate new job creation. It specifically targeted businesses in urban and rural depressed areas and authorized $4.5 million annually over four years for vocational training programs.
- The 1963 amendments to the National Defense Education Act included $731 million in appropriations to states and localities maintaining vocational training programs.

Health

- In 1963, Kennedy, who had a mentally ill sister named Rosemary, submitted the nation's first Presidential special message to Congress on mental health issues. Congress quickly passed the Mental Retardation Facilities and Community Mental Health Centers Construction Act (P.L. 88-164), beginning a new era in Federal support for mental health services. The National Institute of Mental Health assumed responsibility for monitoring community mental health centers programs. This measure was a great success as there was a sixfold increase in people using Mental Health facilities.
- A Medical Health Bill for the Aged (later known as Medicare) was proposed, but Congress failed to enact it.
- The Community Health Services and Facilities Act (1961) increased the amount of funds available for nursing home construction and extended the research and demonstration grant program to other medical facilities.
- The Health Services for Agricultural Migratory Workers Act (1962) established "a program of federal grants for family clinics and other health services for migrant workers and their families".
- The first major amendments to the food and drug safety laws since 1938 were carried out. The Drug Amendments of 1962 amended the Food, Drug and Cosmetic Act (1938) by strengthening the provisions related to the regulation of therapeutic drugs. The Act required evidence that new drugs proposed for marketing were both safe and effective, and required improved manufacturing processes and procedures.

- The responsibilities of the Food and Drug Administration were significantly enlarged by the Kefauver-Harris Drug Amendments (1962).
- The Vaccination Assistance Act (1962) provided for the vaccination of millions of children against a number of diseases.
- The Social Security Act Amendments of 1963 improved medical services for disabled children and established a new project grant program to improve prenatal care for women from low-income families with very high risks of mental disability and other birth defects. Authorizations for grants to the states under the Maternal and Child Health and Crippled Children's programs were also increased and a research grant program was added.
- The Mental Retardation Facilities Construction Act of 1963 authorized federal support for the construction of university-affiliated training facilities, mental disability research centers, and community service facilities for adults and children with mental disability.

{*Author's Note: There is no doubt that many of these programs needed to be passed, especially in the area of mental illness. It is too bad the private sector does not see its responsibility in this area; if they did, the government would not have to step in with entitlement programs.*}

Equal rights for women

- The Presidential Commission on the Status of Women was an advisory commission established on December 14, 1961, by Kennedy to investigate questions regarding women's equality in education, in the workplace, and under the law. The commission, chaired by Eleanor Roosevelt until her death in 1962, was composed of 26 members including legislators, labor union activists and philanthropists who were active in women's rights issues. The main purpose of the committee was to document and examine employment policies in place for women. The commission's final report, *American Woman* (also known as the *Peterson Report* after the Commission's second chair, Esther Peterson), was issued in October 1963 and documented widespread discrimination against women in the workplace. Among the practices addressed by the group were labor laws pertaining to hours and wages, the quality of legal representation for women, the lack of education and counseling for working women, and federal insurance and tax laws that affected women's incomes. Recommendations included affordable child care for all income levels, hiring practices that promoted equal opportunity for women, and paid maternity leave.

- The commission, reflecting the views of Roosevelt and the labor unions, opposed the Equal Rights Amendment.
- In early 1960s, full-time working women were paid on average 59 percent of the earnings of their male counterparts. In order to eliminate some forms of sex-based pay discrimination, Kennedy signed the Equal Pay Act into law on June 10, 1963. During the law's first ten years, 171,000 employees received back pay totaling about 84 million dollars.

Environment

- The Clean Air Act (1963) expanded the powers of the federal government in preventing and controlling air pollution.
- The first major additions to the National Park System since 1946 were made, which included the preservation of wilderness areas and a fund for future acquisitions.

- The water pollution prevention program was doubled.
- More aid was provided to localities to combat water pollution.
- The Rivers and Harbors Act of 1962 reiterated and expanded upon "previous authorizations for outdoor recreation."

{Author's Note: The government was forced into a lot of these programs since manufacturers and industry continued to abuse our rivers and natural resources.}

Agriculture

- A new Housing Act of 1961 extended the Farmers Home Administration housing loan assistance for the first time to nonfarm rural residents and providers of low-cost housing for domestic farm laborers. The Farmers Home Administration was therefore able to expand its rural housing loans from less than $70 million to nearly $500 million in 1965, or about enough to provide for 50,000 new or rehabilitated housing units.

{Author's Note: This is a program the private sector should have taken care of. Who is the government to give free housing to workers? Our forefathers did not have the government provide free housing. This is entitlement at its height. If a worker is working and receiving a paycheck, they should pay for their own housing.}

- A 1962 farm bill expanded government food donation programs at home and abroad and provided federal aid to farmers who converted crop land to nonfarm income-producing uses.
- Title III of the Food and Agriculture Act of 1962 consolidated and expanded existing loan programs, thereby providing the Farmers Home Administration

with increased flexibility in helping a broader spectrum of credit-risky farmers to purchase land and amass working capital. In addition, the Farmers Home Administration assumed responsibility for community water system loans.

- Under the Rural Renewal Program of 1962, the USDA provided technical and financial assistance for locally initiated and sponsored programs aimed at ending chronic underemployment and fostering a sound rural economy. Loans were made to local groups to establish small manufacturing plants, to build hospitals, to establish recreation areas, and to carry out similar developmental activities.

Crime

Under Kennedy, the first significant package of anticrime bills since 1934 were passed. The Kennedy Administration's anticrime measures included the Juvenile Delinquency and Youth Offenses Control Act, which was signed into law on September 22, 1961. This program aimed to prevent youth from committing delinquent acts. In 1963, 288 mobsters were brought to trial by a team that was headed by Kennedy's brother, Robert.

{Author's Note: Delinquent crime has continually been on the rise and still is. The answer is not in government programs but in family unity and Christian upbringing. The Churches of all denominations in American have failed our young kids.}

Defense

- The Kennedy administration with its new Secretary of Defense, Robert S. McNamara, gave a strong priority to countering communist political subversion and guerrilla tactics in the "wars of national liberation" to decolonize the Third World, long held in Western vassalage. As well as fighting and winning a nuclear war, the American military was also trained and equipped for counterinsurgency operations. Though the U.S. Army Special Forces had been created in 1952, Kennedy visited the Fort Bragg U.S. Army Special Warfare Center in a blaze of publicity and gave his permission for the Special Forces to adopt the Green Beret. The other services launched their own counterinsurgency forces in 1961; the U.S. Air Force created the 1st Air Commando Group and the U.S. Navy created the Navy Seals.

- The U.S. Military increased in size and faced possible confrontation with the Soviets with the construction of the Berlin Wall in 1961 and with the Cuban Missile Crisis in 1962. American troops were sent to Laos and South Vietnam in increasing numbers. The United States provided a clandestine operation to supply military aid and support to Cuban exiles in the disastrous Bay of Pigs Invasion. *[Wikipedia – New Frontier]*

{Author's Note: Many feel that the Bay of Pigs invasion was a failure because of the United States not properly backing the invasion. There seems to be thoughts that more air support should have been given. There is no doubt President Kennedy's courage on the Cuban Missile Crisis was the height of his career.}

Author's Summary of John F. Kennedy

{*You have to wonder which President was the greatest in starting the Progressive movement. People like Glen Beck like to give Woodrow Wilson credit for this, but as we go on here it seems that President John Kennedy definitely had his hand in it. Although many of his programs had great beneficial value; it was still a vast movement to get Big Brother to control the American people. I do not believe our forefathers intended that. In my reading on the life of Thomas Jefferson that was definitely not the case. My evaluation at this time, I would say, is that Kennedy had as much to do with progressiveness and entitlement as did Woodrow Wilson. But we need to look at President Johnson and his Great Society as well. Some might say that he just carried on with Kennedy's programs, but Johnson is credited with getting more Great Society programs through to fight the war on poverty than any other president.*}

CHAPTER 7

President Johnson's Great Society

The **Great Society** was a set of domestic programs in the United States launched by Democratic President Lyndon B. Johnson in 1964–65. The term was first coined during a 1964 commencement address by President Lyndon B. Johnson at Ohio University and came to represent his domestic agenda. The main goal was the total elimination of poverty and racial injustice.

New major spending programs that addressed education, medical care, urban problems, rural poverty, and transportation were launched during this period. The program and its initiatives were subsequently promoted by him and fellow Democrats in Congress in the 1960s and years following. The Great Society in scope and sweep resembled the New Deal domestic agenda of Franklin D. Roosevelt.

{Author's Note: Johnson attempted to do this at the same time he was fighting the Vietnam War. This could be one of the reasons the Great Society failed.}

Some Great Society proposals were stalled initiatives from John F. Kennedy's New Frontier. Johnson's success depended on his skills of persuasion, coupled with the Democratic landslide victory in the 1964 elections that brought in many new liberals to Congress, making the House of Representatives in 1965 the most liberal House since 1938. In the 88th Congress it was estimated that there were 56 liberals and 44 conservatives in the Senate, and 224 liberals and 211 conservatives in the House. In the 89th Congress it was estimated that there were 59 liberals and 41 conservatives in the Senate, and 267 liberals and 198 conservatives in the House.

Anti-war Democrats complained that spending on the Vietnam War choked off the Great Society. While some of the programs have been eliminated or had their funding reduced, many of them, including Medicare, Medicaid, the Older Americans Act and federal education funding, continue to the present. The Great Society's programs expanded under the administrations of Republican Presidents Richard Nixon and Gerald Ford.

{Author's Note: *Most of these programs were programs started by President Kennedy, and President Johnson had to continue the programs since they did have the backing of Congress; especially after the landslide election of 1964 which created one of the most liberal House of Representatives in history to that time.*

Economic and Social Conditions

Unlike the old New Deal, which was a response to a severe financial and economic calamity, the Great Society initiatives came during a period of rapid economic growth. Kennedy proposed an across-the-board tax cut lowering the top marginal income tax rate in the United States by 20%, from 91% to 71%, which was enacted in February 1964, three months after Kennedy's assassination, under Johnson. The tax cut also significantly reduced marginal rates in the lower brackets as well as for corporations. The gross national product rose 10% in the first year of the tax cut, and economic growth averaged a rate of 4.5% from 1961 to 1968.

GNP increased by 7% in 1964, 8% in 1965, and 9% in 1966. The unemployment rate fell below 5%, and by 1966 the number of families with incomes of $7,000 a year or more had reached 55%, compared with 22% in 1950. In 1968, when John Kenneth Galbraith published a new edition of *The Affluent Society,* the average income of the American family stood at $8,000, double what it had been a decade earlier. *[Wikipedia: Great Society]*

{Author's Note: What President Kennedy proposed and what President Johnson carried out helped the economy. It also helped get people back to work, because at that time the economy needed revitalization. Cutting taxes like this is why some say President Kennedy was a "good Republican". This needed to happen since the baby boomers were now entering into the work force.}

To deal with escalating problems in urban areas, President Johnson got a bill through Congress establishing a Department of Housing and Urban Development. He appointed Robert Weaver, the first African American in the cabinet, to head it. The department would coordinate vastly expanded slum clearance, public housing programs, and economic redevelopment within inner cities. LBJ also pushed through a "highway beautification" act in which Lady Bird had taken an interest. For the elderly, Johnson won passage of Medicare, a program providing federal funding of many health care expenses for senior citizens. The "medically indigent" of any age who could not afford access to health care would be covered under a related "Medicaid" program funded in part by the national government and run by states under their welfare programs.

The War on Poverty

LBJ's call on the nation to wage war on poverty arose from the ongoing concern that America had not done enough to provide socioeconomic opportunities for the underclass. Statistics revealed that although the proportion of the population below the "poverty line" had dropped from 33 to 23 percent between 1947 and 1956, this rate of decline had not continued; between 1956 and 1962, it dropped only 2 percent. Additionally, during the Kennedy years, the actual number of families in poverty had risen. Most ominous of all, the number of children on welfare, which had increased from 1.6 million in 1950 to 2.4 million in 1960, was still going up. Part of the problem involved racial disparities: the unemployment rate among black youth approached 25 percent -- less at that time than the rate for white youths -- though it had been only 8 percent twenty years before.

To remedy this situation, President Kennedy commissioned a domestic program to alleviate the struggles of the poor. Assuming the presidency when Kennedy was assassinated, Johnson decided to continue the effort after he returned from the tragedy in Dallas. One of the most controversial parts of Johnson's domestic program involved this War on Poverty.

Within six months, the Johnson task forces had come up with plans for a "community action program" that would establish an agency—known as a "community action agency" or CAA—in each city and county to coordinate all federal and state programs designed to help the poor. Each CAA was required to have "maximum feasible participation" from residents of the communities being served. The CAAs in turn would supervise agencies providing social services, mental health services, health services, employment services, and so on. In 1964, Congress passed the Economic Opportunity Act, establishing the Office of Economic Opportunity to run this program. Republicans voted in opposition, claiming that the measure would create an administrative nightmare, and that Democrats had not been willing to compromise with them. Thus the War on Poverty began on a sour, partisan note.

{Author's Note: and history shows it did and there was no compromise on the program from the Democrats}.

Soon, some of the local CAAs established under the law became embroiled in controversy. Local community activists wanted to control the agencies and fought against established city and county politician's intent on dominating the boards. Since both groups were important constituencies in the Democratic Party, the "war" over the War on Poverty threatened party stability. President Johnson ordered Vice President Hubert Humphrey to mediate between community groups and "city halls," but the damage was already done. Democrats were sharply divided, with liberals calling for a greater financial commitment -- Johnson was spending about $1 billion annually -- and conservatives calling for more control by established politicians. Meanwhile, Republicans were charging that local CAAs were run by "poverty hustlers" more intent on lining their own pockets than on alleviating the conditions of the poor.

{Author's Note: This goes on to further indicate that the government cannot control the population by just putting more money into more agencies. When this occurs, it becomes a source for corruption, and this occurred under this agency.}

By 1967, Congress had given local governments the option to take over the CAAs, which significantly discouraged tendencies toward radicalism within the Community Action Program. By the end of the Johnson presidency, more than 1,000 CAAs were in operation, and the number remained relatively constant into the twenty-first century, although their funding and administrative structures were dramatically altered -- they largely became limited vehicles for social service delivery.

{Author's Note: Many believed that these agencies wasted a lot of money on administrative duties and the help never got to the communities.}

Nevertheless, other War on Poverty initiatives have fared better. These include the Head Start program of early education for poor children, the Legal Services Corporation, providing legal aid to poor families; and various health care programs run out of neighborhood clinics and hospitals. *[UVA Miller Center.org – Lyndon B. Johnson: Domestic Affairs]*

Race

Grave social crisis confronted the nation. Racial segregation persisted throughout the South. The Civil Rights Movement was gathering momentum, and in 1964 urban riots began within black neighborhoods in New York City and Los Angeles; by 1968 hundreds of cities had major riots that caused a severe conservative political backlash. *{Author's note: In my traveling to University of Hartford I had to travel through the North End neighborhoods. I thought I was traveling through a war zone.}*

Foreign affairs were generally quiet except for the Vietnam War, which escalated from limited involvement in 1963 to a large-scale military operation in 1968 that soon overshadowed the Great Society. I don't believe that it was the intent of Martin Luther King for this to happen. But what did the poor want; I believe it went beyond equal rights. Johnson's Agenda was needed in the country, the minorities served in the arm services, died for this country and came home and were treated as secondhand citizens. Although I do not agree that the method of burning cities and causing riots was the right way to get there.

Lyndon Baines Johnson moved quickly to establish himself in the office of the Presidency. Despite his conservative voting record in the Senate, Johnson soon reacquainted himself with his liberal roots. LBJ sponsored the largest reform agenda since Roosevelt's New Deal. *[https://www.ushistory.org*

The aftershock of Kennedy's assassination provided a climate for Johnson to complete the unfinished work of JFK's New Frontier. He had eleven months before the election of 1964 to prove to American voters that he deserved a chance to Two very important pieces of legislation were passed. First, the Civil Rights Bill that JFK promised to sign was passed into law. The Civil Rights Act banned discrimination based on race and gender in employment and ending segregation in all public facilities.

Two very important pieces of legislation were passed. First, the **Civil Rights Bill** that JFK promised to sign was passed into law. The Civil Rights Act banned discrimination based on race and gender in employment and ending segregation in all public facilities.

Johnson also signed the omnibus **ECONOMIC OPPORTUNITY ACT OF 1964**. The law created the Office of Economic Opportunity aimed at attacking the roots of American poverty. A Job Corps was established to provide valuable vocational training.

Head Start, a preschool program designed to help disadvantaged students arrive at kindergarten ready to learn was put into place. The **VOLUNTEERS IN SERVICE TO AMERICA**

(VISTA) was set up as a domestic Peace Corps. Schools in impoverished American regions would now receive volunteer teaching attention. Federal funds were sent to struggling communities to attack unemployment and illiteracy.

{Author's Note: As chairperson for the Advisory Committee for the Board of Education in Southington, CT the committee did a study on the Head Start Program, and I have to say the intention of the program was admirable but failed to do what it was supposed to do to help. There was too much red tape and the money usually going to the Board of Education from the federal government sometimes did not go entirely where it was supposed to, which is normal in government distribution of funds. It turned out to be an entitlement program and the criteria to who needed help really didn't totally materialize.}

As he campaigned in 1964, Johnson declared a "war on poverty." He challenged Americans to build a "Great Society" that eliminated the troubles of the poor. Johnson won a decisive victory over his archconservative Republican opponent, Barry Goldwater of Arizona.

{Author's Note: Looking back, the American had no idea what the war on poverty meant. Barry Goldwater was also a Hawk who wanted to expand the Vietnam war more than it already was.}

American liberalism was at high tide under President Johnson.

- The Wilderness Protection Act saved 9.1 million acres of forestland from industrial development.
- The Elementary and Secondary Education Act provided major funding for American public schools.
- The Voting Rights Act banned literacy tests and other discriminatory methods of denying suffrage to African Americans.
- Medicare was created to offset the costs of health care for the nation's elderly.
- The National Endowment for the Arts and Humanities used public money to fund artists and galleries.

- The Immigration Act ended discriminatory quotas based on ethnic origin.
- An Omnibus Housing Act provided funds to construct low-income housing.
- Congress tightened pollution controls with stronger Air and Water Quality Acts.
- Standards were raised for safety in consumer products.

The Civil Rights Act of 1964 was part of Lyndon B. Johnson's "Great Society" reform package — the largest social improvement agenda by a President since FDR's "New Deal." Here, Johnson signs the Civil Rights Act into law before a large audience at the White House. *[https://www.ushistory.org]*

Johnson was an accomplished legislator and used his connections in Congress and forceful personality to pass his agenda.

By 1966, Johnson was pleased with the progress he had made. But soon events in Southeast Asia began to overshadow his domestic achievements. Funds he had envisioned to fight his war on poverty were now diverted to the war in Vietnam. He found himself maligned by conservatives for his domestic policies, and by liberals for his hawkish stance on Vietnam.

{Author's Note: The Vietnam war actually started back with President Kennedy sending so-called "advisors" to the South Vietnamese Army changed the events in the U.S. and the priority of where funds were going to be distributed.}

By 1968, hopes of leaving a legacy of domestic reform were in serious jeopardy. https://www.ushistory.org

{Author's Note: President Johnson now felt his legacy for domestic reform was in danger of never happening. It is also my understanding President Johnson was able to pass more bills through Congress than any President before him and after him.}

Summary of Lyndon B. Johnson

Whatever President Johnson's policies were, he mainly carried on mostly with what President Kennedy had started for domestic programs. His Domestic Policy where he declared the "War on Poverty" was, in many ways, the Kennedy Policies, except President Johnson had more time to carry the programs out. The problem is that the Vietnam War, as mentioned previously, took away a lot of the money that was ear marked for domestic issues.

{Author's Note: President Reagan once said that President Johnson declared the War on Poverty and Poverty won. I believe what he meant by that is that Liberals and Progressives can pour all the money they want into poverty, but it will not solve the problem; you need to elevate the individual, train them and give them something that will raise their self-esteem. Many may disagree, but under President Obama the poverty level increased even further which we will discuss further under the section on President Obama and his "Distribution of Wealth."}

President Johnson did consider the War on Poverty the oldest of ancient mankind's enemies. Some economists, including Milton Friedman, have argued that Johnson's policies actually had a negative impact on the economy because of their interventionist nature; he noted (in *Capitalism and Freedom, published in 1962*) that "the government sets out to eliminate poverty, it has a war on poverty, so-called "poverty" increases." It has a welfare program, and the welfare program leads to an expansion of problems. A general attitude develops that government doesn't have a very efficient way of doing things. Adherents of this school of thought recommend that the best way to fight poverty is not through government spending but through economics.

{Author's Note: The problem is that liberals and progressive seems to think the more money you throw at programs the more successful they would be. Over and over again the liberals have attempted this approach and they always fail. The reason they use this approach is that it is political, and it gets them more votes.

The people voting don't care where the money came from - it only matters that they are getting something for nothing. With the continual progressive and liberal programs from the Wilson years, the trend is towards a more liberal society where the population is relying more and more on the government to give them what they have not earned.}

CHAPTER 8

President Clinton's Silent Liberalism

The Clinton Administration has embarked on the most energetic antipoverty effort in a generation, but it has deliberately done much of it so quietly that few people have noticed.

In an era of painfully tight budgets, the Administration added tens of billions of dollars to existing programs, a major example being the $21 billion expansion of tax credits for low-wage workers.

The Administration has also created a host of new housing, training, and community development programs, which cost less than the tax credits but could set new policy directions for the poor. And while its plans to overhaul welfare and health care faced big hurdles in Congress, they would be landmark antipoverty developments. Taking the Opposite Tack.

In another era, a Democratic White House might have pointed to such efforts to advertise its concern for the needy. But loathe to invite unflattering comparisons to past antipoverty campaigns, officials in the Clinton White House take the opposite tack, bending over backward to frame their actions as part of an effort to help the broad middle class.

{_Author's Note: The positive thing about the Clinton years is that since FDR we have had the lowest unemployment and the lowest inflation in many years. One of the things not mentioned so far in the book titled The Agenda by Bob Woodward is the women behind the President. In the case of President Clinton,_ *he had Hilary Clinton, a diehard progressive liberal. Not only did he have a secretive antipoverty program going, but he also had his wife pushing for a National Health Care program. She wasn't successful, but she was pushing hard for it.}*

While the Administration did highlight the tax credit expansion, for instance, officials described it more as an attempt to help workers than as a major onslaught against poverty.

In talks with a half-dozen top antipoverty officials, the word "poverty" scarcely comes up. Instead, there is talk about "children," "work," "investments" and "empowerment."

{Author's Note: Empowerment is another way of getting around a program by letting folks think they are being done a favor (from their view point), but they are not being done a favor, because the "favor" (program) is another form of liberalism.}

"We don't term things a lot around here as antipoverty," said Carol Rasco, the White House domestic policy advisor. "But from the get-go we've talked about work."

{Author's Note: It's funny how politicians can word things so it doesn't sound like liberalism and that it really isn't costing anything because they are helping individuals get something else for nothing!}

Most Administration officials say it would be counterproductive for President Clinton to talk too much about the poorest Americans, particularly the black and Hispanic residents of violent ghettos. Middle-Class Backlash Feared

They say it could provoke a backlash from middle-class voters who would interpret his remarks, regardless of the specifics, as a call for higher taxes and a return to failed government programs.

{Author's Note: This was his way of keeping his progressive movement form the public. The press, continually becoming very liberal, played his game.}

The negative imagery associated with the "war on poverty" under President Lyndon B. Johnson is so great that most antipoverty strategists endorse the middle-class wrappings, with only an occasional rueful complaint that the nation is ignoring its racial and class conflicts.

The oratorical caution is not absolute, of course, and it may have started to give way. Mr. Clinton gave a major speech about poverty and violence ... in Memphis, and he returned to the theme of ghetto poverty ... when he visited a junior high school in Washington.

[https://www.nytimes.com/1994/03/30/us/clinton-wages-a-quiet-war-against-poverty.html]

{Author's Note: This is all happening when President Clinton is promising a balanced budget What great political strategy. This was a time when BOTH parties, especially the Republicans led by New Gingrich, also wanted a balanced budget. For the first time in a century, both parties worked together to balance a budget by the time the next election in the year 2000 came around.}

Then .... a series of Cabinet officials will outline domestic efforts at different conferences, which were sponsored by the Department of Housing and Urban Development for about 2,000 people who run housing and development programs.

In videotaped remarks, the President will praise their efforts "to battle poverty and cynicism." And a draft of the keynote address, by Vice President Al Gore, indicates that he will use the speech to define the Administration's urban agenda. He argues that the programs amount to a "powerful approach to breathe new life into distressed communities."

The list of initiatives is long and varied. Some programs focus on needy places, like the plan to spend $3 billion over five years on empowerment zones. *{Author's Note: And there is the work empowerment again, a great progressive liberal word.}* The program will give tax breaks and social service grants to 10 poor neighborhoods with promising revitalization strategies.

[https://www.nytimes.com/1994/03/30/us/clinton-wages-a-quiet-war-against-poverty.html]

Bill Clinton Summary

The Clinton administration got off to a shaky start, the victim of what some critics called ineptitude and bad judgment. His attempt to fulfill a campaign promise to end discrimination against gay men and lesbians in the military was met with criticism from conservatives and some military leaders—including Gen. Colin Powell, the chairman of the Joint Chiefs of Staff. In response, Clinton proposed a compromise policy—summed up by the phrase "Don't ask, don't tell"—that failed to satisfy either side of the issue. Clinton's first two nominees for attorney general withdrew after questions were raised about domestic workers they had hired. Clinton's efforts to sign campaign-finance reform legislation were quashed by a Republican filibuster in the Senate, as was his economic-stimulus package.

Clinton had promised during the campaign to institute a system of universal health insurance. His appointment of his wife to chair the Task Force on National Health Care Reform, a novel role for the country's first lady, was criticized by conservatives, who objected both to the propriety of the arrangement and to Hillary Rodham Clinton's feminist views. They joined lobbyists for the insurance industry, small-business organizations, and the American Medical Association to campaign vehemently against the task force's eventual proposal, the Health Security Act. Despite protracted negotiations with Congress, all efforts to pass compromise legislation failed.

Despite these early missteps, Clinton's first term was marked by numerous successes, including the passage by Congress of the North American Free Trade Agreement, which created a free-trade zone for the United States, Canada, and Mexico. Clinton also appointed several women and minorities to significant government posts throughout his administration, including Janet Reno as attorney general, Donna Shalala as secretary of Health and Human Services, Joycelyn Elders as surgeon general, Madeleine Albright as the first woman secretary of state, and Ruth Bader Ginsburg as the second woman justice on the United States Supreme Court. During Clinton's first term, Congress enacted a deficit-reduction package—which passed the Senate with a tie-breaking vote from Gore—and some 30 major bills related to education, crime prevention, the environment, and women's and family issues, including the Violence Against Women Act and the Family and Medical Leave Act.

In January 1994 Attorney General Reno approved an investigation into business dealings by Clinton and his wife with an Arkansas housing development corporation known as Whitewater. Led from August by independent counsel Kenneth Starr, the Whitewater inquiry consumed several years and more than $50 million but did not turn up conclusive evidence of wrongdoing by the Clintons.

The renewal of the Whitewater investigation under Starr, the continuing rancorous debate in Congress over Clinton's health care initiative, and the liberal character of some of Clinton's policies—which alienated significant numbers of American voters—all contributed to Republican electoral victories in November 1994, when the party gained a majority in both houses of Congress for the first time in 40 years. A chastened Clinton subsequently tempered some of his policies and accommodated some Republican proposals, eventually embracing a more aggressive deficit-reduction plan and a massive overhaul of the country's welfare system while continuing to oppose Republican efforts to cut government spending on social programs. Ultimately, most American voters found themselves more alienated by the uncompromising and confrontational behaviour of the new Republicans in Congress than they had been by Clinton, who won considerable public sympathy for his more moderate approach.

Clinton's initiatives in foreign policy during his first term included a successful effort in September–October 1994 to reinstate Haitian Pres. Jean-Bertrand Aristide, who had been ousted by a military coup in 1991; the sponsorship of peace talks and the eventual Dayton Accords (1995) aimed at ending the ethnic conflict in Bosnia and Herzegovina; and a leading role in the ongoing attempt to bring about a permanent resolution of the dispute between Palestinians and Israelis. In 1993 he invited Israeli Prime Minister Yitzhak Rabin and Palestine Liberation Organization chairman Yasser Arafat to Washington to sign a historic agreement that granted limited Palestinian self-rule in the Gaza Strip and Jericho.

Although scandal was never far from the White House—a fellow Arkansan who had been part of the administration committed suicide; there were rumours of financial irregularities that had occurred in Little Rock; former associates were indicted and convicted of crimes; and rumours of sexual impropriety involving the president persisted—Clinton was handily reelected in 1996, buoyed by a recovering and increasingly strong economy. He captured 49 percent of the popular vote to Republican Bob Dole's 41 percent and Perot's 8 percent; the electoral vote was 379 to 159. Strong economic growth continued during Clinton's second term, eventually setting a record for the country's longest peacetime expansion. By 1998 the Clinton administration was overseeing the first balanced budget since 1969 and the largest budget surpluses in the country's history. The vibrant economy also produced historically high levels of home ownership and the lowest unemployment rate in nearly 30 years.

In 1998 Starr was granted permission to expand the scope of his continuing investigation to determine whether Clinton had encouraged a 24-year-old White House intern, Monica Lewinsky, to state falsely under oath that she and Clinton had not had an affair. Clinton repeatedly and publicly denied that the affair had taken place. His compelled testimony, which appeared evasive and disingenuous even to Clinton's supporters (he responded to one question by stating, "It depends on what the meaning of the word is is"), prompted renewed criticism of Clinton's character from conservatives and liberals alike. After conclusive evidence of the affair came to light, Clinton apologized to his family and to the American public. On the basis of Starr's 445-page report and supporting evidence, the House of Representatives in 1998 approved two articles of impeachment, for perjury and obstruction of justice. Clinton was acquitted of the charges by the Senate in 1999. Despite his impeachment, Clinton's job-approval rating remained high.

In foreign affairs, Clinton ordered a four-day bombing campaign against Iraq in December 1998 in response to Iraq's failure to cooperate fully with United Nations weapons inspectors (the bombing coincided with the start of full congressional debate on Clinton's impeachment). In 1999 U.S.-led forces of the North Atlantic Treaty Organization (NATO) conducted a successful three-month bombing campaign against Yugoslavia designed to end Serbian attacks on ethnic Albanians in the province of Kosovo. In 1998 and 2000 Clinton was hailed as a peacemaker in visits to Ireland and Northern Ireland, and in 2000 he became the first U.S. president to visit Vietnam since the end of the Vietnam War. He spent the last weeks of his presidency in an unsuccessful effort to broker a final peace agreement between the Israelis and the Palestinians. Shortly before he left office, Clinton was roundly criticized by Democrats as well as by Republicans for having issued a number of questionable pardons, including one to the former spouse of a major Democratic Party contributor. *[https://www.britannica.com/biography/Bill-Clinton/Presidency]*

CHAPTER 9

President George Bush: The War

President Bush's administration was not one of a progressive movement or one of a lot of social programs. Shortly after he came into office the country was faced with the terrorist attack of September 11, 2001. This was when 19 al-Qaeda Islamic terrorists attacked and took down the twin financial towers of the World Trade Center in New York. Along with those two attacks, they also attacked the Pentagon and the airline that was taken down in Shanksville, PA. That day over 3000 American lives and lives of people from countries were taken.

President Bush's administration was at war and after discovering Osama bin Laden was responsible the full resources of the American economy was focused on eliminating bin Laden and any future terrorist attack. It was discovered that the country responsible for harboring the terrorist was Afghanistan. The United States, with many of our allies - especially New Britain - put together a military force to eliminate bin Laden and the terrorists in Afghanistan. This was to be a continual war that totally engulfed his 8 years in office.

It was then we learned that there were many terrorists in the country of Iraq. The coalition then decided to also invade Iraq and eliminate the terrorists there. Then in March of 2003, the United States invaded Iraq. This drained more of our resources, since before Bush got elected president the military in the United States was not at the capacity to handle a war against one country, let along two. At that time President Bush had to build up the military which raised our military budget to over 700 trillion dollars. This was the largest United States military budget ever.

President Bush's 8 years in office was a time of going after terrorists. Not only did he have to be concerned about fighting the terrorists in Afghanistan and Iraq, but also about protecting the United States against domestic terrorists in this country who went after our own citizens.

One of the departments he set up was Homeland Security in order to have a law enforcement organization which would look out for the United States. One of the security programs that was also created under Homeland Security was the TSA at airports. Previously, when a passenger wanted to get on an airline, they bought a ticket and went to the terminal and checked in. Now a passenger had to go through a security line where their baggage and personal items had to be checked for weapons. It went as far as taking off your shoes and putting them through a radar detection device and then the individual had to walk through a detection tube to make sure he was safe to get on the airplane. This insured that all passengers would be safe and secure, and this process continues today. The inspections by the TSA worked because we have never had a serious incident in the country since then.

So, in the years President Bush was in office, it was spent concentrating on protecting the country. I have to say during that time there was a rise in patriotism as there was during WWII. Many men signed up for the military. But as in any war a lot of young service people died leaving many families without their loved ones.

CHAPTER 10

Barack Obama and Social Entitlement

There have been discrepancies on where President Obama was born, his religious belief if there is one, and on whether he is a Muslim. But the discussion here is not about those issues. It is about whether or not he is a Progressive Socialist. Although he ran on the Democratic ticket, he does not resemble the Democratic Party as we knew it in the days of John Kennedy. Many say, and I would have to agree, that in today's political sphere, President Kennedy would make a good Republican. I even remember what I was doing the moment I heard he had gotten shot. It was a very sad day in American history.

As I mentioned, I am not sure we can say in this chapter that President Obama was acting as a Democrat. Many of us feel he was a socialist, with income distribution and more, in creating more big government than any other Democratic president before him. His background in Chicago was as a community organizer. Let us be honest --they thrive on the government helping them and giving them everything. His wife Michele is from the same background. Questions have arisen on how he got through college and who paid for it, although this is not important to the subject being discussed here. Did he feel life owes him and he intends to collect? The point is that all of a sudden, a basically unknown from Chicago gets elected as a Senator from Chicago, and after one term gets elected as President of the strongest country in the world, and the most economically strong country in the world. Someone had to be behind him from the start. We do know at this point that he believes in income distribution and taking it from the "haves" and giving it to the "have-nots". His health program, called ObamaCare, reflects that and will be further discussed.

Unemployment when Obama took office in 2009, was slightly under 6%; in 2010 it went to almost 10% and then in 2013 approximately 7.3%. Population on entitlement programs when Obama left office was approximately 47%. That figure takes in Social Security which is not right. These elderly folks have earned that income by paying into Social Security for their entire working lives, and it is not right to include them in the list of entitlement programs. It would seem to me that those of us who had money taken from our paychecks for their entire work history, deserve to receive it back, therefore is not receiving entitlement money. It is not our fault that President Johnson decided to take those dollars from the Social Security Trust Fund to wage his war in Vietnam and his war on poverty, replacing them with IOUs. Nobody in Congress talks about the Social Security that never got paid back or about those IOU's. So, the real number on entitlement is approximately 34% taking out the Social Security benefits. *[Statistics from Facttank News in Numbers]*

The poverty and unemployment levels among Blacks have risen a couple of percentage points also since Obama had been president. Salaries among Blacks have decreased, so why do the Blacks think he is so great besides him being the first Black president? And it is sad, regardless of your race, that someone votes for an individual solely _because_ of his race. Obama's background is an indication of how he thinks. A person's environment and how he was raised will carry him through his life; especially in Obama's case since he stayed in that environment with the people he associated with. *[as noted in "2016: Obama's America - Dinesh D'Souza (Director), John Sullivan (Director)"--]*

Let us look at the areas that we will discuss here which, in my opinion, makes President Obama the King of the

Progressives way beyond President Wilson or even President Franklin Roosevelt. We will look at:

a. Food stamps
b. Welfare entitlement
c. Poverty level
d. Unemployment
e. Distribution of Unemployment checks
f. Federal Debts

Food Stamps

The number of people receiving food stamps continued at record levels. The number of people in the United States receiving Food Stamps 47,760,285 in December of 2013 was estimated to be closer to 49,000,000 (2013 is the most recent figure reported by the U.S. Department of Agriculture). That's an increase of more than 200,000 since the July 2013 update. The latest figures represent an increase of 49.3 percent since the day Obama first took office -- about 3 percentage points higher than our first report a year ago. *[These figures were taken from the 2013 White House Fact Sheet]*

{*Author's Note: Many of Obama's staff and constituents like to blame President Bush for the state of the economy and the increase in entitlements, but the fact is that "buck-passing" can only hold for the first year or maybe two of the next President's term. After a while it is old hat. As we've noted previously, the increase under Obama is due mainly to the economic downturn that began in late 2007, but also mostly due to Obama's signing legislation to increase benefit levels and to allow able-bodied single persons to receive food stamps.*}

In 2004, food stamp recipients totaled approximately 9 million and by 2013 it was nearly 49 million! Granted, a lot of this was also created under President Bush, but since 2007 food stamps recipients went up 70%. And the total has remained historically high even as the economy has improved, and as the

90

unemployment rate has declined substantially. If approximately 49,000,000 are on food stamps, that is 15 percent of the entire U.S. population remaining on food stamps. The U.S. cannot continue to sustain this type of Progressive Entitlement.

Beyond politics, equally large (or larger) gaps emerge in the participation rates of many core social and demographic groups. For example, women were about twice as likely as men (23% vs. 12%) to have received food stamps at some point in their lives. Blacks are about twice as likely as Whites to have used this benefit during their lives (31% vs. 15%). Among Hispanics, about 22% say they have collected food stamps. *[Stephen Dinan - The Washington Times - Thursday, October 18, 2012]*

Minority women in particular are far more likely than their male counterparts to have used food stamps. About four-in-ten Black women (39%) have gotten help compared with 21% of Black men. The gender-race participation gap is also wide among Hispanics: 31% of Hispanic women but 14% of Hispanic men received assistance. Among Whites, the gender-race gap is smaller. Still, White women are about twice as likely as White men to receive food stamp assistance (19% vs. 11%). *[Statistics from Facttank News in Numbers]*

{Author's Note: From these statistics, it could be concluded that Obama wanted to live up to his promise of income distribution by taxing more "haves" and giving it to the "have-nots" who, in the first place did not want to work for it and do not know what to do with it.}

Welfare entitlement

The Washington Times reported much of the following on Welfare spending, and it sums up what happened under the Obama administration in Washington.

Federal welfare spending has grown by 32 percent over the past four years, fattened by President Obama's stimulus spending and swelled by a growing number of Americans whose recession-depleted incomes now qualify them for public assistance, according to numbers released Thursday.

Federal spending on more than 80 low-income assistance programs reached $746 billion in 2011, and state spending on those programs brought the total to $1.03 trillion, according to figures from the Congressional Research Service and the Senate Budget Committee.

That makes welfare the single biggest chunk of federal spending — topping Social Security and basic defense spending.

Sen. Jeff Sessions, the ranking Republican on the Budget Committee who requested the Congressional Research Service report, said the numbers underscore a fundamental shift in welfare, which he said has moved from being a Band-Aid and toward a more permanent crutch.

"No longer should we measure compassion by how much money the government spends but by how many people we help to rise out of poverty." The Alabama conservative said. "Welfare assistance should be seen as temporary whenever possible, and the goal must be to help more of our fellow citizens attain gainful employment and financial independence."

Welfare spending, as measured by obligations stood at $563 billion in fiscal year 2008, but reached $746 billion in fiscal year 2011, a jump of 32 percent. *[By Stephen Dinan - The Washington Times - Thursday, October 18, 2012]*

{Author's Note: The question is -- where do we go from here? Sooner, rather than later, we will bankrupt ourselves. Do you or anyone else believe the rich and upper middle class will continue letting the government tax them? I don't think so!!}

The numbers tell a complex story of American taxpayers' generosity in supporting a varied social safety net, including food stamps, support for low-income AIDS patients, childcare payments and direct cash going from taxpayers to the poor.

{Author's Note: Or will it come to an end by the Washington politicians or some other means? Under the Obama Administration, these numbers continued to grow. His health care program,

*which is a failure, continues to sign low income Americans up for
Medicaid which is an insurance for the low income taxpayers.}*

By far, the biggest item on the list is Medicaid, the federal-
state health care program for the poor, which at $296 billion in
federal spending made up 40 percent of all low-income assistance
in 2011. That total was up $82 billion from 2008 *{Author's Note:
and continues to grow!}.*

*{Author's Note: Next is a great one which Obama has
handed out to the poor like it was candy.}*

Beyond that, the next big program Food Stamps $75
billion in 2011, or 10 percent of welfare spending. It is nearly twice
the size it was in 2008 and accounts for a staggering 20 percent
of the total welfare spending increase of those four years

*{Author's Note: This is the income distribution that Obama
was talking about and the middle class fell for it and now they are
being taxed by their favorite person.}*

Several programs to funnel cash to the poor also ranked
high. Led by the earned income tax credit, supplemental security
income and the additional child tax credit, direct cash aid
accounts for about a fifth of all welfare.

Mr. Sessions' staff on the Senate Budget Committee
calculated that states contributed another $283 billion to low-
income assistance — chiefly through Medicaid.

Richard Kogan, senior fellow at the liberal-leaning Center
on Budget and Policy Priorities, said that while the dollar amounts
for low-income assistance are growing, they still represent about
the same slice of the budget pie when viewed over the long run.
*{Author's Note: For that to be true that means to have that slice,
more tax money was attributed to the low-income assistance.}*
He said the costs may have spiked during the recession, but are
projected to drop back to more normal levels once the economy
recovers.

*{Author's Note: As Senator Ted Cruz, from Texas said, "Have
you ever seen an entitlement program reduced or eliminated?"
Of course, he was referring to ObamaCare when he made the
statement, but it does hold true to any entitlement program.}*

As for Medicaid, where major spending increases have been made, Mr. Kogan said even there it may be a savings. "Medicaid provides health care at a noticeably cheaper price than Medicare does, and both are cheaper than the cost of private-sector health insurance," he said. "The problem is not that the programs are badly designed — it is that the entire health care system in the U.S. is much more expensive than in any other advanced country."

Combined with several programs also directed at health care, the category made up 46 percent of total welfare spending in 2011.

"Virtually all the rest is in the form of in-kind assistance: Medicaid, SNAP, WIC, housing vouchers, Pell Grants, LIHEAP and childcare vouchers; or in the form of direct services, such as community health centers, Title 1 education, foster care, school lunch and Head Start," he said.

Rather than straight transfers, those other programs provide support for services Congress has deemed worthy of funding. SNAP is the Supplemental Nutrition Assistance Program that used to be called Food Stamps; LIHEAP is the Low Income Home Energy Assistance Program; WIC is the Women, Infants and Children nutrition program; and Pell Grants provide assistance for college costs.

The conservative Heritage Foundation said roughly 100 million Americans get benefits from at least one low-income assistance program each month, with the average benefit coming to around $9,000.

The think tank estimates that if welfare spending were transferred as straight cash instead, it would be five times more than needed to lift every American family above the poverty line — though many of the programs help those above the poverty line. *{Author's Note: If you look at this overall picture you have to be brain dead not to ask, 'Where are we going with this?"}*

Mr. Sessions' Budget Committee staff said that at current projections, the 10 biggest welfare programs will cost $8.3 trillion over the next decade.

{Author's Note: At the rate that President Obama was going this might be a conservative estimate. He was cutting military and whatever other programs he could to put more money into entitlement. Is he not wanting to create a socialistic entitlement state - taking away the ability and integrity of the individual to make it on their own?}

The Congressional Research Service looked at obligations for each program as its measure of spending. It included every program that had eligibility requirements that seemed designed chiefly to benefit those with lower or limited incomes. The report looked at programs that had obligations of at least $100 million in a fiscal year, which meant some small-dollar welfare assistance wasn't included.

Political Wrangle

The report was released as President Obama and Republican presidential nominee Mitt Romney fight over the size and scope of government assistance.

Mr. Obama has taken heat from Republicans for a new policy that Republicans argued would remove work requirements from the 1996 welfare reform. The administration said it is merely adding more flexibility for states, which still would have to prove the law is meeting its jobs goals.

Mr. Romney was damaged last month by caught-on-camera remarks in which he said 47 percent of Americans are dependent on government and see themselves as victims.

{Author's Note: Although he was telling the truth, the liberal media was just waiting for Mr. Romney to make statements that they could run with and use against him. The American people don't want the truth, just what makes them comfortable to hear.}

In Tuesday's debate, Mr. Romney blasted Mr. Obama for overseeing a 50 percent increase in the number of people on Food Stamps, which has risen from 32 million to 47 million.

[https://m.washingtontimes.com/news/2012/oct/18/welfare-spending-jumps-32-percent-four-years/]

{*Author's Note: Again, I don't think the American people understand where this money comes from to support these programs. They must think there is a money tree in Washington DC. I guess there is -- the Federal Reserve prints it as they want to.*}

The Affordable Care Act a/k/a ObamaCare

Let us understand that the ACA program is not doing what it was intended to do. But by the same token, something was going to happen eventually. The insurance companies have had a free ride in the U.S. to do what they want and charge what they want. Individuals would go to hospital and get an outrageous bill and people would blame the hospital (although some may have been their fault), while others would blame the insurance company. I am not for socialized medicine, but I am for helping folks who cannot afford these outrageous bills.

Let's discuss what the ACA program does for you and then we will go over what this is costing and whether it is really working. The ACA program improved the benefits you receive in ten ways.

1. 20 million fewer Americans are uninsured;
2. The ACA protects people with preexisting conditions from discrimination.
3. Medicaid expansion helped millions of lower income individuals access heal care and more;
4. Health care became affordable;
5. Women can no longer be charged more for insurance and are guaranteed coverage for services essential to women's health;
6. Young adults and children have greater access to coverage;
7. The ACA improved access to prescription drugs;
8. Rural communities have benefited from the ACA;
9. The ACA lowered costs for seniors on Medicare;
10. Protections for disabled people were enhanced.

*[https://www.americanprogress.org/issues/healthcare/
news/2020/03/23/482012/10-ways-aca-improved-health-care-
past-decade/]*

Let us look at what has happened since the entitlement program has taken effect.

a. Approx.7 million insured individuals have had their insurance cancelled due to the guidelines of the Affordable Care Act.
b. 7 million had to be signed up by the end of March 2014; although at that point approximately 7 million had registered and who knows how many of those have actually gotten insurance or how many have really paid their premiums. Many of these have signed up for Medicaid which it is understood approx. 3 million have. What is wrong with this Medicaid is that it is an entitlement program which the government receives no money for. How much will this ACA program wind up costing the taxpayers before our legislatures wake up?
c. Obama said this would save an average of $2500 per year for family insurance cost. Instead, it has cost family's thousands more per year.
d. Insurance cost has gone up and doctors have dropped out of insurance programs, and some have even retired from their practice.

The Eighty-three percent of American physicians have considered leaving their practices over President Barack Obama's health care reform law, according to a survey released by the *Doctor Patient Medical Association*," the Daily Caller reported.

The DPMA, a non-partisan association of doctors and patients, surveyed a random selection of 699 doctors nationwide. The survey found that the majority thought about bailing out of their careers over the legislation.

Even if no doctors quit, the U.S. will face a shortage of at least 90,000 doctors by 2020, the estimates. Five years after that, the shortage will be 130,000. *[https://tylerpaper.com/opinion/ editorials/doctor-shortages-will-limit-access/article_277fdafc-4acf-5214-8fb4-8193d8f5793c.html]*

A recent report from the Association of Medical Colleges projects doctor shortages of up to 121,300 within the next 12 years. That's a 16% increase from their forecast just last year. *[https://www.investors.com/politics/editorials/ doctor-shortages-obamacare-ehr/]*

{*Author's Note: The ACA law increased demand for physicians by expanding insurance coverage. This change will exacerbate the current shortage as more Americans live past 65. And beyond this, you don't have the options of choosing your own doctor, due to your need to find one that will accept the ACA program. Another example of the problem with the ACA program is how it will be paid for, and who is going to pay for it? Well, I have experienced that personally. My co-pay for my insurance at the pharmacy has tripled. When I asked the pharmacist, he told me it was because of ObamaCare or the ACA program. It is sad when the retired or elderly individuals in this country have to pay for an entitlement program out of money that they have spent their life earning. I don't believe there has been an indication that someone's health care costs have been reduced because of the introduction of ACA.*

President Obama claimed that Republicans were busy probing "phony scandals." But the sheer number of scandals in his administration suggested that misbehavior, abuse of power, and possibly corruption are not something being dreamed up by the GOP, but a defining characteristic of the Obama Administration.}

Valerie Jarrett, President Obama's chief adviser and family friend, proudly announced Monday that his administration had been scandal free during his eight years in office. Breitbart News, however, disagreed and presented a short list of 18 scandals. Herewith an excerpt of its list:

1. *The great "stimulus" heist*: Mr. Obama grabbed almost trillion dollars for "stimulus" spending, but created virtually zero private-sector jobs, allowed a great deal of the money to vanish and spent the rest of his presidency complaining he needed hundreds of billions more to repair roads and bridges.

2. *Operation Fast and Furious*: Mr. Obama's insane program to use American gun dealers and straw purchasers to arm Mexican drug lords so the administration could complain about lax regulations on American gun sales to restrict American Second Amendment constitutional rights. Border Patrol Agent Brian Terry and Immigration and Customs Enforcement Agent Jamie Zapata, plus hundreds of Mexican citizens, died as a result of the blotched operation. Attorney General Eric Holder escaped charges claiming he didn't know what his subordinates were doing.

3. *Eric Holder held in contempt of Congress*: Because of Operation of Fast and Furious. the White House, Democrats and the press protected him. Mr. Holder said it was "politically motivated."

4. *ObamaCare*: ObamaCare would not be affordable said Jonathan Gruber, Ph.D., MIT professor of economics and chief architect of ObamaCare which passed March 23, 2010, without any Republican vote.

5. *Spying on journalists*: AP reporters and James Rosen of Fox News, etc.

6. *The IRS scandal*: Selective targeting of conservative groups, i.e., pro-life and Tea Party groups, by a politicized IRS, denying tax exempt status. IRS officials lied allowing scandal kingpin Lois Lerner to retire taxpayer funded.

7. *Benghazi*: In a failed attempt to send arms to Syrian rebels, four Americans died because Mr. Obama, Secretary of State Hillary Clinton refused to send help. They then lied about the cause of the attack for

weeks afterward, prompting Mrs. Clinton to ask "What difference at this point does it make?"

8. *Hillary Clinton's secret server*: Subverting rules, she was guilty of sending classified email on her home-brew server, and Mr. Obama knew about it.

9. *The Pigford scandal*: Abuse of a program using taxpayer dollars meant to compensate minority farmers for racial discrimination exploded.

10. *NSA spying scandal*: Edward Snowden's pilfering of sensitive National Security Agency data damaged national security, creating diplomatic problems and AG Eric Holder thanked Mr. Snowden for performing a public service by exposing surveillance programs the Obama administration didn't want to talk about.

11. *Sgt. Bowe Bergdahl*: He left his post, went over to the Taliban, soldiers died looking for him, yet Mr. Obama traded five high profile Taliban prisoners for him, flouting the law and lying.

12. *Iran nuclear deal and ransom payment*: Pushed with lies and media manipulation, Mr. Obama allowed Iran to pursue nuclear power, paying it billions of taxpayer dollars to use for worldwide terrorism.

13. *Polluting the Colorado River*: The Environmental Protection Agency turned the river orange unleashing water from closed copper mines. EPA officials escaped punishment.

14. *GSA scandal*: General Services Administration wasted taxpayer money on lavish parties; the administration tried to cover it up.

15. *VA death list scandal*: Department of Veterans Affairs put veterans on secret death lists and executives turned in phony status reports and signed themselves up for big bonuses. Mr. Obama spun the news with hollow promises.

16. *Solyndra*: The green energy scandal wrote "crony capitalism" into the American political lexicon, cutting corners and wasting $535 million of tax dollars.

17. *Secret Service gone wild*: White House fence jumpers, tipsy Secret Service agents driving a car into a security barrier and agents soliciting hookers in Columbia.

18. *Shutdown theater*: During the government shutdown of 2013, Mr. Obama did everything he could to make citizens feel maximum pain, from barricades to keep veterans away from memorials, to releasing illegal alien criminals from detention centers — an infuriating lesson for voters in how every dollar they get from government is a dollar that can be used against them when are they impudent enough to demand spending restraint.

[https://www.carolinacoastonline.com/news_times/opinions/ editorials/article_574cf49e-d2b8-11e6-8960-ab7b13d83409.html]

{*Author's Note: Some may ask, "What do these scandals have to do with Liberalism or the Progressive Movement in the United States"? It makes no difference what the scandal; is in their Liberal Progressive philosophy Liberals and Progressives don't feel they have to answer for anything. It is as if the Liberals and Progressives believe that everything they think or feel is what the people in American want, totally forgetting everything that the founding fathers stood for. These scandals in the Progressive Movement wind up costing the taxpayers money and takes away from properly running the country.*

If you examine these scandals, they mostly have a theme of entitlement attached to them. The IRS scandal is targeting folks who want less government and less giving away of their tax dollars or want to pay less in taxes, which in turn would result in less entitlement. Granted, many of these scandals mentioned above are more political than entitlement related. However, they still take away from the real issue at hand which is that the taxpayer is paying too much in taxes in order to subsidize a potential welfare state. As I write this the numbers are continually changing. So, if they are different when you read this book, my apologies to the reader. Continual overspending by the government will do that.

In conclusion in discussing President Obama, it could be debated whether he did good or not in attempting to have a health care system for everyone. The big question is why there were so many scandals during his administration that was covered up by the press. It is no secret in this country that the press leans to the liberal's side of politics. It seems that if a Republican does something illegal or unethical, it gets smashed all over the front page, but not when a liberal does something illegal or unethical.

Writer Keith Koffler mentioned why, with so many scandals during Obama's presidency, Democrats still and other many Americans praise President Obama. One thing you can say is that while he was President, he did represent himself as a great family man for his wife and two girls. Only history will say whether he do that great of a job as the first Black President.}

CHAPTER 11

Donald Trump - The Outsider President

In the 2016 election, the country elected a president who was not from the Washington swamp and who, in his personal life, was not a politician, although in running his real estate empire he had to use a lot of politics with others to become a multi-billionaire. This man was Donald Trump. He said he would clean out the swamp, but his challenge was more of the Democratic Party who would not accept him as President and who did all they could to take him down. While fighting that, he achieved the following:

Unprecedented Economic Boom

Before the China Virus invaded our shores, we built the world's most prosperous economy.

- America gained 7 million new jobs – more than three times government experts' projections.
- Middle-Class family income increased nearly $6,000 – more than five times the gains during the entire previous administration.
- The unemployment rate reached 3.5 percent, the lowest in a half-century.
- Achieved 40 months in a row with more job openings than job-hirings.

- More Americans reported being employed than ever before – nearly 160 million.
- Jobless claims hit a nearly 50-year low.
- The number of people claiming unemployment insurance as a share of the population hit its lowest on record.
- Incomes rose in every single metro area in the United States for the first time in nearly 3 decades.

Delivered a future of greater promise and opportunity for citizens of all backgrounds.

- Unemployment rates for African Americans, Hispanic Americans, Asian Americans, Native Americans, veterans, individuals with disabilities, and those without a high school diploma all reached record lows.
- Unemployment for women hit its lowest rate in nearly 70 years.
- Lifted nearly 7 million people off of food stamps.
- Poverty rates for African Americans and Hispanic Americans reached record lows.
- Income inequality fell for two straight years, and by the largest amount in over a decade.
- The bottom 50 percent of American households saw a 40 percent increase in net worth.
- Wages rose fastest for low-income and blue collar workers – a 16 percent pay increase.
- African American homeownership increased from 41.7 percent to 46.4 percent.

Brought jobs, factories, and industries back to the USA.

- Created more than 1.2 million manufacturing and construction jobs.

- Put in place policies to bring back supply chains from overseas.
- Small business optimism broke a 35-year old record in 2018.

Hit record stock market numbers and record 401ks.

- The DOW closed above 20,000 for the first time in 2017 and topped 30,000 in 2020.
- The S&P 500 and NASDAQ have repeatedly notched record highs.

Rebuilding and investing in rural America.

- Signed an Executive Order on Modernizing the Regulatory Framework for Agricultural Biotechnology Products, which is bringing innovative new technologies to market in American farming and agriculture.
- Strengthened America's rural economy by investing over $1.3 billion through the Agriculture Department's ReConnect Program to bring high-speed broadband infrastructure to rural America.

Achieved a record-setting economic comeback by rejecting blanket lockdowns.

- An October 2020 Gallup survey found 56 percent of Americans said they were better off during a pandemic than four years prior.
- During the third quarter of 2020, the economy grew at a rate of 33.1 percent – the most rapid GDP growth ever recorded.
- Since coronavirus lockdowns ended, the economy has added back over 12 million jobs, more than half the jobs lost.

- Jobs have been recovered 23 times faster than the previous administration's recovery.
- Unemployment fell to 6.7 percent in December, from a pandemic peak of 14.7 percent in April – beating expectations of well over 10 percent unemployment through the end of 2020.
- Under the previous administration, it took 49 months for the unemployment rate to fall from 10 percent to under 7 percent compared to just 3 months for the Trump Administration.
- Since April, the Hispanic unemployment rate has fallen by 9.6 percent, Asian-American unemployment by 8.6 percent, and Black American unemployment by 6.8 percent.
- 80 percent of small businesses are now open, up from just 53 percent in April.
- Small business confidence hit a new high.
- Homebuilder confidence reached an all-time high, and home sales hit their highest reading since December 2006.
- Manufacturing optimism nearly doubled.
- Household net worth rose $7.4 trillion in Q2 2020 to $112 trillion, an all-time high.
- Home prices hit an all-time record high.
- The United States rejected crippling lockdowns that crush the economy and inflict countless public health harms and instead safely reopened its economy.
- Business confidence is higher in America than in any other G7 or European Union country.
- Stabilized America's financial markets with the establishment of a number of Treasury Department supported facilities at the Federal Reserve.

Tax Relief for the Middle Class

Passed $3.2 trillion in historic tax relief and reformed the tax code.

- Signed the Tax Cuts and Jobs Act – the largest tax reform package in history.
- More than 6 million American workers received wage increases, bonuses, and increased benefits thanks to the tax cuts.
- A typical family of four earning $75,000 received an income tax cut of more than $2,000 – slashing their tax bill in half.
- Doubled the standard deduction – making the first $24,000 earned by a married couple completely tax-free.
- Doubled the child tax credit.
- Virtually eliminated the unfair Estate Tax, or Death Tax.
- Cut the business tax rate from 35 percent – the highest in the developed world – all the way down to 21 percent.
- Small businesses can now deduct 20 percent of their business income.
- Businesses can now deduct 100 percent of the cost of their capital investments in the year the investment is made.
- Since the passage of tax cuts, the share of total wealth held by the bottom half of households has increased, while the share held by the top 1 percent has decreased.
- Over 400 companies have announced bonuses, wage increases, new hires, or new investments in the United States.
- Over $1.5 trillion was repatriated into the United States from overseas.
- Lower investment cost and higher capital returns led to faster growth in the middle class, real wages, and international competitiveness.

Jobs and investments are pouring into Opportunity Zones.

- Created nearly 9,000 Opportunity Zones where capital gains on long-term investments are taxed at zero.
- Opportunity Zone designations have increased property values within them by 1.1 percent, creating an estimated $11 billion in wealth for the nearly half of Opportunity Zone residents who own their own home.
- Opportunity Zones have attracted $75 billion in funds and driven $52 billion of new investment in economically distressed communities, creating at least 500,000 new jobs.
- Approximately 1 million Americans will be lifted from poverty as a result of these new investments.
- Private equity investments into businesses in Opportunity Zones were nearly 30 percent higher than investments into businesses in similar areas that were not designated Opportunity Zones.

Massive Deregulation

Ended the regulatory assault on American Businesses and Workers.

- Instead of 2-for-1, we eliminated 8 old regulations for every 1 new regulation adopted.
- Provided the average American household an extra $3,100 every year.
- Reduced the direct cost of regulatory compliance by $50 billion, and will reduce costs by an additional $50 billion in FY 2020 alone.
- Removed nearly 25,000 pages from the Federal Register – more than any other president. The previous administration added over 16,000 pages.

- Established the Governors' Initiative on Regulatory Innovation to reduce outdated regulations at the state, local, and tribal levels.
- Signed an executive order to make it easier for businesses to offer retirement plans.
- Signed two executive orders to increase transparency in Federal agencies and protect Americans and their small businesses from administrative abuse.
- Modernized the National Environmental Policy Act (NEPA) for the first time in over 40 years.
- Reduced approval times for major infrastructure projects from 10 or more years down to 2 years or less.
- Helped community banks by signing legislation that rolled back costly provisions of Dodd-Frank.
- Established the White House Council on Eliminating Regulatory Barriers to Affordable Housing to bring down housing costs.
- Removed regulations that threatened the development of a strong and stable internet.
- Eased and simplified restrictions on rocket launches, helping to spur commercial investment in space projects.
- Published a whole-of-government strategy focused on ensuring American leadership in automated vehicle technology.
- Streamlined energy efficiency regulations for American families and businesses, including preserving affordable lightbulbs, enhancing the utility of showerheads, and enabling greater time savings with dishwashers.
- Removed unnecessary regulations that restrict the seafood industry and impede job creation.

- Modernized the Department of Agriculture's biotechnology regulations to put America in the lead to develop new technologies.
- Took action to suspend regulations that would have slowed our response to COVID-19, including lifting restrictions on manufacturers to more quickly produce ventilators.

Successfully rolled back burdensome regulatory overreach.

- Rescinded the previous administration's Affirmatively Furthering Fair Housing (AFFH) rule, which would have abolished zoning for single-family housing to build low-income, federally subsidized apartments.
- Issued a final rule on the Fair Housing Act's disparate impact standard.
- Eliminated the Waters of the United States Rule and replaced it with the Navigable Waters Protection Rule, providing relief and certainty for farmers and property owners.
- Repealed the previous administration's costly fuel economy regulations by finalizing the Safer Affordable Fuel Efficient (SAFE) Vehicles rule, which will make cars more affordable, and lower the price of new vehicles by an estimated $2,200.

Americans now have more money in their pockets.

- Deregulation had an especially beneficial impact on low-income Americans who pay a much higher share of their incomes for overregulation.
- Cut red tape in the healthcare industry, providing Americans with more affordable healthcare and saving Americans nearly 10 percent on prescription drugs.

- Deregulatory efforts yielded savings to the medical community an estimated $6.6 billion – with a reduction of 42 million hours of regulatory compliance work through 2021.
- Removed government barriers to personal freedom and consumer choice in healthcare.
- Once fully in effect, 20 major deregulatory actions undertaken by the Trump Administration are expected to save American consumers and businesses over $220 billion per year.
- Signed 16 pieces of deregulatory legislation that will result in a $40 billion increase in annual real incomes.

Fair and Reciprocal Trade

Secured historic trade deals to defend American workers.

- Immediately withdrew from the job-killing Trans-Pacific Partnership (TPP).
- Ended the North American Free Trade Agreement (NAFTA), and replaced it with the brand new United States-Mexico-Canada Agreement (USMCA).
- The USMCA contains powerful new protections for American manufacturers, auto-makers, farmers, dairy producers, and workers.
- The USMCA is expected to generate over $68 billion in economic activity and potentially create over 550,000 new jobs over ten years.
- Signed an executive order making it government policy to Buy American and Hire American, and took action to stop the outsourcing of jobs overseas.
- Negotiated with Japan to slash tariffs and open its market to $7 billion in American agricultural products and ended its ban on potatoes and lamb.

- Over 90 percent of American agricultural exports to Japan now receive preferential treatment, and most are duty-free.
- Negotiated another deal with Japan to boost $40 billion worth of digital trade.
- Renegotiated the United States-Korea Free Trade Agreement, doubling the cap on imports of American vehicles and extending the American light truck tariff.
- Reached a written, fully enforceable Phase One trade agreement with China on confronting pirated and counterfeit goods, and the protection of American ideas, trade secrets, patents, and trademarks.
- China agreed to purchase an additional $200 billion worth of United States exports and opened market access for over 4,000 American facilities to exports while all tariffs remained in effect.
- Achieved a mutual agreement with the European Union (EU) that addresses unfair trade practices and increases duty-free exports by 180 percent to $420 million.
- Secured a pledge from the EU to eliminate tariffs on American lobster – the first United States-European Union negotiated tariff reduction in over 20 years.
- Scored a historic victory by overhauling the Universal Postal Union, whose outdated policies were undermining American workers and interests.
- Engaged extensively with trade partners like the EU and Japan to advance reforms to the World Trade Organization (WTO).
- Issued a first-ever comprehensive report on the WTO Appellate Body's failures to comply with WTO rules and interpret WTO agreements as written.
- Blocked nominees to the WTO's Appellate Body until WTO Members recognize and address longstanding issues with Appellate Body activism.
- Submitted 5 papers to the WTO Committee on Agriculture to improve Members' understanding of

how trade policies are implemented, highlight areas for improved transparency, and encourage members to maintain up-to-date notifications on market access and domestic support.

Took strong actions to confront unfair trade practices and put America First.

- Imposed tariffs on hundreds of billions worth of Chinese goods to protect American jobs and stop China's abuses under Section 232 of the Trade Expansion Act of 1962 and Section 301 of the Trade Act of 1974.
- Directed an all-of-government effort to halt and punish efforts by the Communist Party of China to steal and profit from American innovations and intellectual property.
- Imposed tariffs on foreign aluminum and foreign steel to protect our vital industries and support our national security.
- Approved tariffs on $1.8 billion in imports of washing machines and $8.5 billion in imports of solar panels.
- Blocked illegal timber imports from Peru.
- Took action against France for its digital services tax that unfairly targets American technology companies.
- Launched investigations into digital services taxes that have been proposed or adopted by 10 other countries.

Historic support for American farmers.

- Successfully negotiated more than 50 agreements with countries around the world to increase foreign market access and boost exports of American agriculture products, supporting more than 1 million American jobs.

- Authorized $28 billion in aid for farmers who have been subjected to unfair trade practices – fully funded by the tariffs paid by China.
- China lifted its ban on poultry, opened its market to beef, and agreed to purchase at least $80 billion of American agricultural products in the next two years.
- The European Union agreed to increase beef imports by 180 percent and opened up its market to more imports of soybeans.
- South Korea lifted its ban on American poultry and eggs, and agreed to provide market access for record exports of American rice.
- Argentina lifted its ban on American pork.
- Brazil agreed to increase wheat imports by $180 million a year and raised its quotas for purchases of United States ethanol.
- Guatemala and Tunisia opened up their markets to American eggs.
- Won tariff exemptions in Ecuador for wheat and soybeans.
- Suspended $817 million in trade preferences for Thailand under the Generalized System of Preferences (GSP) program due to its failure to adequately provide reasonable market access for American pork products.
- The amount of food stamps redeemed at farmers markets increased from $1.4 million in May 2020 to $1.75 million in September 2020 – a 50 percent increase over last year.
- Rapidly deployed the Coronavirus Food Assistance Program, which provided $30 billion in support to farmers and ranchers facing decreased prices and market disruption when COVID-19 impacted the food supply chain.
- Authorized more than $6 billion for the Farmers to Families Food Box program, which delivered over 128 million boxes of locally sourced, produce, meat, and

dairy products to charity and faith-based organizations nationwide.

- Delegated authorities via the Defense Production Act to protect breaks in the American food supply chain as a result of COVID-19.

American Energy Independence

Unleashed America's oil and natural gas potential.

- For the first time in nearly 70 years, the United States has become a net energy exporter.
- The United States is now the number one producer of oil and natural gas in the world.
- Natural gas production reached a record-high of 34.9 quads in 2019, following record high production in 2018 and in 2017.
- The United States has been a net natural gas exporter for three consecutive years and has an export capacity of nearly 10 billion cubic feet per day.
- Withdrew from the unfair, one-sided Paris Climate Agreement.
- Canceled the previous administration's Clean Power Plan, and replaced it with the new Affordable Clean Energy rule.
- Approved the Keystone XL and Dakota Access pipelines.
- Opened up the Arctic National Wildlife Refuge (ANWR) in Alaska to oil and gas leasing.
- Repealed the last administration's Federal Coal Leasing Moratorium, which prohibited coal leasing on Federal lands.
- Reformed permitting rules to eliminate unnecessary bureaucracy and speed approval for mines.

- Fixed the New Source Review permitting program, which punished companies for upgrading or repairing coal power plants.
- Fixed the Environmental Protection Agency's (EPA) steam electric and coal ash rules.
- The average American family saved $2,500 a year in lower electric bills and lower prices at the gas pump.
- Signed legislation repealing the harmful Stream Protection Rule.
- Reduced the time to approve drilling permits on public lands by half, increasing permit applications to drill on public lands by 300 percent.
- Expedited approval of the NuStar's New Burgos pipeline to export American gasoline to Mexico.
- Streamlined Liquefied natural gas (LNG) terminal permitting and allowed long-term LNG export authorizations to be extended through 2050.
- The United States is now among the top three LNG exporters in the world.
- Increased LNG exports five-fold since January 2017, reaching an all-time high in January 2020.
- LNG exports are expected to reduce the American trade deficit by over $10 billion.
- Granted more than 20 new long-term approvals for LNG exports to non-free trade agreement countries.
- The development of natural gas and LNG infrastructure in the United States is providing tens of thousands of jobs, and has led to the investment of tens of billions of dollars in infrastructure.
- There are now 6 LNG export facilities operating in the United States, with 2 additional export projects under construction.
- The amount of nuclear energy production in 2019 was the highest on record, through a combination of increased capacity from power plant upgrades and shorter refueling and maintenance cycles.

- Prevented Russian energy coercion across Europe through various lines of effort, including the Partnership for Transatlantic Energy Cooperation, civil nuclear deals with Romania and Poland, and opposition to Nord Stream 2 pipeline.
- Issued the Presidential Permit for the A2A railroad between Canada and Alaska, providing energy resources to emerging markets.

Increased access to our country's abundant natural resources in order to achieve energy independence.

- Renewable energy production and consumption both reached record highs in 2019.
- Enacted policies that helped double the amount of electricity generated by solar and helped increase the amount of wind generation by 32 percent from 2016 through 2019.
- Accelerated construction of energy infrastructure to ensure American energy producers can deliver their products to the market.
- Cut red tape holding back the construction of new energy infrastructure.
- Authorized ethanol producers to sell E15 year-round and allowed higher-ethanol gasoline to be distributed from existing pumps at filling stations.
- Ensured greater transparency and certainty in the Renewable Fuel Standard (RFS) program.
- Negotiated leasing capacity in the Strategic Petroleum Reserve to Australia, providing American taxpayers a return on this infrastructure investment.
- Signed an executive order directing Federal agencies to work together to diminish the capability of foreign adversaries to target our critical electric infrastructure.
- Reformed Section 401 of the Clean Water Act regulation to allow for the curation of interstate infrastructure.

- Resolved the OPEC (Organization of the Petroleum Exporting Countries) oil crisis during COVID-19 by getting OPEC, Russia, and others to cut nearly 10 million barrels of production a day, stabilizing world oil prices.
- Directed the Department of Energy to use the Strategic Petroleum Reserve to mitigate market volatility caused by COVID-19.

Investing in America's Workers and Families

Affordable and high-quality Child Care for American workers and their families.

- Doubled the Child Tax Credit from $1,000 to $2,000 per child and expanded the eligibility for receiving the credit.
- Nearly 40 million families benefitted from the child tax credit (CTC), receiving an average benefit of $2,200 – totaling credits of approximately $88 billion.
- Signed the largest-ever increase in Child Care and Development Block Grants – expanding access to quality, affordable child care for more than 800,000 low-income families.
- Secured an additional $3.5 billion in the Coronavirus Aid, Relief, and Economic Security (CARES) Act to help families and first responders with child care needs.
- Created the first-ever paid family leave tax credit for employees earning $72,000 or less.
- Signed into law 12-weeks of paid parental leave for Federal workers.
- Signed into law a provision that enables new parents to withdraw up to $5,000 from their retirement accounts without penalty when they give birth to or adopt a child.

Advanced apprenticeship career pathways to good-paying jobs.

- Expanded apprenticeships to more than 850,000 and established the new Industry-Recognized Apprenticeship programs in new and emerging fields.
- Established the National Council for the American Worker and the American Workforce Policy Advisory Board.
- Over 460 companies have signed the Pledge to America's Workers, committing to provide more than 16 million job and training opportunities.
- Signed an executive order that directs the Federal government to replace outdated degree-based hiring with skills-based hiring.

Advanced women's economic empowerment.

- Included women's empowerment for the first time in the President's 2017 National Security Strategy.
- Signed into law key pieces of legislation, including the Women, Peace, and Security Act and the Women Entrepreneurship and Economic Empowerment Act.
- Launched the Women's Global Development and Prosperity (W-GDP) Initiative – the first-ever whole-of-government approach to women's economic empowerment that has reached 24 million women worldwide.
- Established an innovative new W-GDP Fund at USAID.
- Launched the Women Entrepreneurs Finance Initiative (We-Fi) with 13 other nations.
- Announced a $50 million donation on behalf of the United States to We-Fi providing more capital to women-owned businesses around the world.

- Released the first-ever Strategy on Women, Peace, and Security, which focused on increasing women's participation to prevent and resolve conflicts.
- Launched the W-GDP 2x Global Women's Initiative with the Development Finance Corporation, which has mobilized more than $3 billion in private sector investments over three years.

Ensured American leadership in technology and innovation.

- First administration to name artificial intelligence, quantum information science, and 5G communications as national research and development priorities.
- Launched the American Broadband Initiative to promote the rapid deployment of broadband internet across rural America.
- Made 100 megahertz of crucial mid-band spectrum available for commercial operations, a key factor to driving widespread 5G access across rural America.
- Launched the American AI Initiative to ensure American leadership in artificial intelligence (AI), and established the National AI Initiative Office at the White House.
- Established the first-ever principles for Federal agency adoption of AI to improve services for the American people.
- Signed the National Quantum Initiative Act establishing the National Quantum Coordination Office at the White House to drive breakthroughs in quantum information science.
- Signed the Secure 5G and Beyond Act to ensure America leads the world in 5G.
- Launched a groundbreaking program to test safe and innovative commercial drone operations nationwide.
- Issued new rulemaking to accelerate the return of American civil supersonic aviation.

- Committed to doubling investments in AI and quantum information science (QIS) research and development.
- Announced the establishment of $1 billion AI and quantum research institutes across America.
- Established the largest dual-use 5G test sites in the world to advance 5G commercial and military innovation.
- Signed landmark Prague Principles with America's allies to advance the deployment of secure 5G telecommunications networks.
- Signed first-ever bilateral AI cooperation agreement with the United Kingdom.
- Built collation among allies to ban Chinese Telecom Company Huawei from their 5G infrastructure.

Preserved American jobs for American workers and rejected the importation of cheap foreign labor.

- Pressured the Tennessee Valley Authority (TVA) to reverse their decision to lay off over 200 American workers and replace them with cheaper foreign workers.
- Removed the TVA Chairman of the Board and a TVA Board Member.

Life-Saving Response to China Virus

Restricted travel to the United States from infected regions of the world.

- Suspended all travel from China, saving thousands of lives.
- Required all American citizens returning home from designated outbreak countries to return through designated airports with enhanced screening measures, and to undergo a self-quarantine.

- Announced further travel restrictions on Iran, the Schengen Area of Europe, the United Kingdom, Ireland, and Brazil.
- Issued travel advisory warnings recommending that American citizens avoid all international travel.
- Reached bilateral agreements with Mexico and Canada to suspend non-essential travel and expeditiously return illegal aliens.
- Repatriated over 100,000 American citizens stranded abroad on more than 1,140 flights from 136 countries and territories.
- Safely transported, evacuated, treated, and returned home trapped passengers on cruise ships.
- Took action to authorize visa sanctions on foreign governments who impede our efforts to protect American citizens by refusing or unreasonably delaying the return of their own citizens, subjects, or residents from the United States.

Acted early to combat the China Virus in the United States.

- Established the White House Coronavirus Task Force, with leading experts on infectious diseases, to manage the Administration's efforts to mitigate the spread of COVID-19 and to keep workplaces safe.
- Pledged in the State of the Union address to "take all necessary steps to safeguard our citizens from the Virus," while the Democrats' response made not a single mention of COVID-19 or even the threat of China.
- Declared COVID-19 a National Emergency under the Stafford Act.
- Established the 24/7 FEMA National Response Coordination Center.
- Released guidance recommending containment measures critical to slowing the spread of the Virus,

decompressing peak burden on hospitals and infrastructure, and diminishing health impacts.

- Implemented strong community mitigation strategies to sharply reduce the number of lives lost in the United States down from experts' projection of up to 2.2 million deaths in the United States without mitigation.
- Halted American funding to the World Health Organization to counter its egregious bias towards China that jeopardized the safety of Americans.
- Announced plans for withdrawal from the World Health Organization and redirected contribution funds to help meet global public health needs.
- Called on the United Nations to hold China accountable for their handling of the virus, including refusing to be transparent and failing to contain the virus before it spread.

Re-purposed domestic manufacturing facilities to ensure frontline workers had critical supplies.

- Distributed billions of pieces of Personal Protective Equipment, including gloves, masks, gowns, and face shields.
- Invoked the Defense Production Act over 100 times to accelerate the development and manufacturing of essential material in the USA.
- Made historic investments of more than $3 billion into the industrial base.
- Contracted with companies such as Ford, General Motors, Philips, and General Electric to produce ventilators.
- Contracted with Honeywell, 3M, O&M Halyard, Moldex, and Lydall to increase our Nation's production of N-95 masks.

- The Army Corps of Engineers built 11,000 beds, distributed 10,000 ventilators, and surged personnel to hospitals.
- Converted the Javits Center in New York into a 3,000-bed hospital, and opened medical facilities in Seattle and New Orleans.
- Dispatched the USNS Comfort to New York City, and the USNS Mercy to Los Angeles.
- Deployed thousands of FEMA employees, National Guard members, and military forces to help in the response.
- Provided support to states facing new emergences of the virus, including surging testing sites, deploying medical personnel, and advising on mitigation strategies.
- Announced Federal support to governors for use of the National Guard with 100 percent cost-share.
- Established the Supply Chain Task Force as a "control tower" to strategically allocate high-demand medical supplies and PPE to areas of greatest need.
- Requested critical data elements from states about the status of hospital capacity, ventilators, and PPE.
- Executed nearly 250 flights through Project Air Bridge to transport hundreds of millions of surgical masks, N95 respirators, gloves, and gowns from around the world to hospitals and facilities throughout the United States.
- Signed an executive order invoking the Defense Production Act to ensure that Americans have a reliable supply of products like beef, pork, and poultry.
- Stabilized the food supply chain restoring the Nation's protein processing capacity through a collaborative approach with Federal, state, and local officials and industry partners.
- The continued movement of food and other critical items of daily life distributed to stores and to American homes went unaffected.

Replenished the depleted Strategic National Stockpile.

- Increased the number of ventilators nearly ten-fold to more than 153,000.
- Despite the grim projections from the media and governors, no American who has needed a ventilator has been denied a ventilator.
- Increased the number of N95 masks fourteen-fold to more than 176 million.
- Issued an executive order ensuring critical medical supplies are produced in the United States.

Created the largest, most advanced, and most innovative testing system in the world.

- Built the world's leading testing system from scratch, conducting over 200 million tests – more than all of the European Union combined.
- Engaged more than 400 test developers to increase testing capacity from less than 100 tests per day to more than 2 million tests per day.
- Slashed red tape and approved Emergency Use Authorizations for more than 300 different tests, including 235 molecular tests, 63 antibody tests, and 11 antigen tests.
- Delivered state-of-the-art testing devices and millions of tests to every certified nursing home in the country.
- Announced more flexibility to Medicare Advantage and Part D plans to waive cost-sharing for tests.
- Over 2,000 retail pharmacy stores, including CVS, Walmart, and Walgreens, are providing testing using new regulatory and reimbursement options.
- Deployed tens of millions of tests to nursing homes, assisted living facilities, historically black colleges and universities (HBCUs), tribes, disaster relief operations,

Home Health/Hospice organizations, and the Veterans Health Administration.

- Began shipping 150 million BinaxNOW rapid tests to states, long-term care facilities, the IHS, HBCUs, and other key partners.

Pioneered groundbreaking treatments and therapies that reduced the mortality rate by 85 percent, saving over 2 million lives.

- The United States has among the lowest case fatality rates in the entire world.
- The Food and Drug Administration (FDA) launched the Coronavirus Treatment Acceleration Program to expedite the regulatory review process for therapeutics in clinical trials, accelerate the development and publication of industry guidance on developing treatments, and utilize regulatory flexibility to help facilitate the scaling-up of manufacturing capacity.
- More than 370 therapies are in clinical trials and another 560 are in the planning stages.
- Announced $450 million in available funds to support the manufacturing of Regeneron's antibody cocktail.
- Shipped tens of thousands of doses of the Regeneron drug.
- Authorized an Emergency Use Authorization (EUA) for convalescent plasma.
- Treated around 100,000 patients with convalescent plasma, which may reduce mortality by 50 percent.
- Provided $48 million to fund the Mayo Clinic study that tested the efficacy of convalescent plasma for patients with COVID-19.
- Made an agreement to support the large-scale manufacturing of AstraZeneca's cocktail of two monoclonal antibodies.

- Approved Remdesivir as the first COVID-19 treatment, which could reduce hospitalization time by nearly a third.
- Secured more than 90 percent of the world's supply of Remdesivir, enough to treat over 850,000 high-risk patients.
- Granted an EUA to Eli Lilly for its anti-body treatments.
- Finalized an agreement with Eli Lilly to purchase the first doses of the company's investigational antibody therapeutic.
- Provided up to $270 million to the American Red Cross and America's Blood Centers to support the collection of up to 360,000 units of plasma.
- Launched a nationwide campaign to ask patients who have recovered from COVID-19 to donate plasma.
- Announced Phase 3 clinical trials for varying types of blood thinners to treat adults diagnosed with COVID-19.
- Issued an EUA for the monoclonal antibody therapy bamlanivimab.
- FDA issued an EUA for casirivimab and imdevimab to be administered together.
- Launched the COVID-19 High Performance Computing Consortium with private sector and academic leaders unleashing America's supercomputers to accelerate coronavirus research.

Brought the full power of American medicine and government to produce a safe and effective vaccine in record time.

- Launched Operation Warp Speed to initiate an unprecedented drive to develop and make available an effective vaccine by January 2021.
- Pfizer and Moderna developed two vaccines in just nine months, five times faster than the fastest prior vaccine development in American history.

- Pfizer and Moderna's vaccines are approximately 95 effective – far exceeding all expectations.
- AstraZeneca and Johnson & Johnson also both have promising candidates in the final stage of clinical trials.
- The vaccines will be administered within 24 hours of FDA-approval.
- Made millions of vaccine doses available before the end of 2020, with hundreds of millions more to quickly follow.
- FedEx and UPS will ship doses from warehouses directly to local pharmacies, hospitals, and healthcare providers.
- Finalized a partnership with CVS and Walgreens to deliver vaccines directly to residents of nursing homes and long-term care facilities as soon as a state requests it, at no cost to America's seniors.
- Signed an executive order to ensure that the United States government prioritizes getting the vaccine to American citizens before sending it to other nations.
- Provided approximately $13 billion to accelerate vaccine development and to manufacture all of the top candidates in advance.
- Provided critical investments of $4.1 billion to Moderna to support the development, manufacturing, and distribution of their vaccines.
- Moderna announced its vaccine is 95 percent effective and is pending FDA approval.
- Provided Pfizer up to $1.95 billion to support the mass-manufacturing and nationwide distribution of their vaccine candidate.
- Pfizer announced its vaccine is 95 percent effective and is pending FDA approval.
- Provided approximately $1 billion to support the manufacturing and distribution of Johnson & Johnson's vaccine candidate.

- Johnson & Johnson's vaccine candidate reached the final stage of clinical trials.
- Made up to $1.2 billion available to support AstraZeneca's vaccine candidate.
- AstraZeneca's vaccine candidate reached the final stage of clinical trials.
- Made an agreement to support the large-scale manufacturing of Novavax's vaccine candidate with 100 million doses expected.
- Partnered with Sanofi and GSK to support large-scale manufacturing of a COVID-19 investigational vaccine.
- Awarded $200 million in funding to support vaccine preparedness and plans for the immediate distribution and administration of vaccines.
- Provided $31 million to Cytvia for vaccine-related consumable products.
- Under the PREP Act, issued guidance authorizing qualified pharmacy technicians to administer vaccines.
- Announced that McKesson Corporation will produce store, and distribute vaccine ancillary supply kits on behalf of the Strategic National Stockpile to help healthcare workers who will administer vaccines.
- Announced partnership with large-chain, independent, and regional pharmacies to deliver vaccines.

Prioritized resources for the most vulnerable Americans, including nursing home residents.

- Quickly established guidelines for nursing homes and expanded telehealth opportunities to protect vulnerable seniors.
- Increased surveillance, oversight, and transparency of all 15,417 Medicare and Medicaid nursing homes by requiring them to report cases of COVID-19 to all residents, their families, and the Centers for Disease Control and Prevention (CDC).

- Required that all nursing homes test staff regularly.
- Launched an unprecedented national nursing home training curriculum to equip nursing home staff with the knowledge they need to stop the spread of COVID-19.
- Delivered $81 million for increased inspections and funded 35,000 members of the Nation Guard to deliver critical supplies to every Medicare-certified nursing homes.
- Deployed Federal Task Force Strike Teams to provide onsite technical assistance and education to nursing homes experiencing outbreaks.
- Distributed tens of billions of dollars in Provider Relief Funds to protect nursing homes, long-term care facilities, safety-net hospitals, rural hospitals, and communities hardest hit by the virus.
- Released 1.5 million N95 respirators from the Strategic National Stockpile for distribution to over 3,000 nursing home facilities.
- Directed the White House Opportunity and Revitalization Council to refocus on underserved communities impacted by the coronavirus.
- Required that testing results reported include data on race, gender, ethnicity, and ZIP code, to ensure that resources were directed to communities disproportionately harmed by the virus.
- Ensured testing was offered at 95 percent of Federally Qualified Health Centers (FQHC), which serve over 29 million patients in 12,000 communities across the Nation.
- Invested an unprecedented $8 billion in tribal communities.
- Maintained safe access for Veterans to VA healthcare throughout the COVID-19 Pandemic and supported non-VA hospital systems and private and state-run nursing homes with VA clinical teams.
- Signed legislation ensuring no reduction of VA education benefits under the GI Bill for online distance learning.

Supported Americans as they safely return to school and work.

- Issued the Guidelines for Opening Up America Again, a detailed blueprint to help governors as they began reopening the country. Focused on protecting the most vulnerable and mitigating the risk of any resurgence, while restarting the economy and allowing Americans to safely return to their jobs.
- Helped Americans return to work by providing extensive guidance on workplace-safety measures to protect against COVID-19, and investigating over 10,000 coronavirus-related complaints and referrals.
- Provided over $31 billion to support elementary and secondary schools.
- Distributed 125 million face masks to school districts.
- Provided comprehensive guidelines to schools on how to protect and identify high-risk individuals, prevent the spread of COVID-19, and conduct safe in-person teaching.
- Brought back the safe return of college athletics, including Big Ten and Pac-12 football.

Rescued the American economy with nearly $3.4 trillion in relief, the largest financial aid package in history.

- Secured an initial $8.3 billion Coronavirus Preparedness and Response Act, supporting the development of treatments and vaccines, and to procure critical medical supplies and equipment.
- Signed the $100 billion Families First Coronavirus Relief Act, guaranteeing free coronavirus testing, emergency paid sick leave and family leave, Medicaid funding, and food assistance.
- Signed the $2.3 trillion Coronavirus Aid, Relief, and Economic Security (CARES) Act, providing

unprecedented and immediate relief to American families, workers, and businesses.

- Signed additional legislation providing nearly $900 billion in support for coronavirus emergency response and relief, including critically needed funds to continue the Paycheck Protection Program.
- Signed the Paycheck Protection Program and Healthcare Enhancement Act, adding an additional $310 billion to replenish the program.
- Delivered approximately 160 million relief payments to hardworking Americans.
- Through the Paycheck Protection Program, approved over $525 billion in forgivable loans to more than 5.2 million small businesses, supporting more than 51 million American jobs.
- The Treasury Department approved the establishment of the Money Market Mutual Fund Liquidity Facility to provide liquidity to the financial system.
- The Treasury Department, working with the Federal Reserve, was able to leverage approximately $4 trillion in emergency lending facilities.
- Signed an executive order extending expanded unemployment benefits.
- Signed an executive order to temporarily suspend student loan payments, evictions, and collection of payroll taxes.
- Small Business Administration expanded access to emergency economic assistance for small businesses, faith-based, and religious entities.
- Protected jobs for American workers impacted by COVID-19 by temporarily suspending several job-related nonimmigrant visas, including H-1B's, H-2B's without a nexus to the food-supply chain, certain H-4's, as well as L's and certain J's.

Greater Healthcare for Americans

Empowered American patients by greatly expanding healthcare choice, transparency, and affordability.

- Eliminated the Obamacare individual mandate – a financial relief to low and middle-income households that made up nearly 80 percent of the families who paid the penalty for not wanting to purchase health insurance.
- Increased choice for consumers by promoting competition in the individual health insurance market leading to lower premiums for three years in a row.
- Under the Trump Administration, more than 90 percent of the counties have multiple options on the individual insurance market to choose from.
- Offered Association Health Plans, which allow employers to pool together and offer more affordable, quality health coverage to their employees at up to 30 percent lower cost.
- Increased availability of short-term, limited-duration health plans, which can cost up to 60 percent less than traditional plans, giving Americans more flexibility to choose plans that suit their needs.
- Expanded Health Reimbursement Arrangements, allowing millions of Americans to be able to shop for a plan of their choice on the individual market, and then have their employer cover the cost.
- Added 2,100 new Medicare Advantage plan options since 2017, a 76 percent increase.
- Lowered Medicare Advantage premiums by 34 percent nationwide to the lowest level in 14 years. Medicare health plan premium savings for beneficiaries have totaled $nearly 1.5 billion since 2017.
- Improved access to tax-free health savings accounts for individuals with chronic conditions.

- Eliminated costly Obamacare taxes, including the health insurance tax, the medical device tax, and the "Cadillac tax."
- Worked with states to create more flexibility and relief from oppressive Obamacare regulations, including reinsurance waivers to help lower premiums.
- Released legislative principles to end surprise medical billing.
- Finalized requirements for unprecedented price transparency from hospitals and insurance companies so patients know what the cost is before they receive care.
- Took action to require that hospitals make the prices they negotiate with insurers publicly available and easily accessible online.
- Improved patients access to their health data by penalizing hospitals and causing clinicians to lose their incentive payments if they do not comply.
- Expanded access to telehealth, especially in rural and underserved communities.
- Increased Medicare payments to rural hospitals to stem a decade of rising closures and deliver enhanced access to care in rural areas.

Issued unprecedented reforms that dramatically lowered the price of prescription drugs.

- Lowered drug prices for the first time in 51 years.
- Launched an initiative to stop global freeloading in the drug market.
- Finalized a rule to allow the importation of prescription drugs from Canada.
- Finalized the Most Favored Nation Rule to ensure that pharmaceutical companies offer the same discounts to the United States as they do to other nations, resulting

in an estimated $85 billion in savings over seven years and $30 billion in out-of-pocket costs alone.

- Proposed a rule requiring federally funded health centers to pass drug company discounts on insulin and Epi-Pens directly to patients.
- Ended the gag clauses that prevented pharmacists from informing patients about the best prices for the medications they need.
- Ended the costly kickbacks to middlemen and ensured that patients directly benefit from available discounts at the pharmacy counter, saving Americans up to 30 percent on brand name pharmaceuticals.
- Enhanced Part D plans to provide many seniors with Medicare access to a broad set of insulins at a maximum $35 copay for a month's supply of each type of insulin.
- Reduced Medicare Part D prescription drug premiums, saving beneficiaries nearly $2 billion in premium costs since 2017.
- Ended the Unapproved Drugs Initiative, which provided market exclusivity to generic drugs.

Promoted research and innovation in healthcare to ensure that American patients have access to the best treatment in the world.

- Signed first-ever executive order to affirm that it is the official policy of the United States Government to protect patients with pre-existing conditions.
- Passed Right To Try to give terminally ill patients access to lifesaving cures.
- Signed an executive order to fight kidney disease with more transplants and better treatment.
- Signed into law a $1 billion increase in funding for critical Alzheimer's research.

- Accelerated medical breakthroughs in genetic treatments for Sickle Cell disease.
- Finalized the interoperability rules that will give American patients access to their electronic health records on their phones.
- Initiated an effort to provide $500 million over the next decade to improve pediatric cancer research.
- Launched a campaign to end the HIV/AIDS epidemic in America in the next decade.
- Started a program to provide the HIV prevention drug PrEP to uninsured patients for free.
- Signed an executive order and awarded new development contracts to modernize the influenza vaccine.

Protected our Nation's seniors by safeguarding and strengthening Medicare.

- Updated the way Medicare pays for innovative medical products to ensure beneficiaries have access to the latest innovation and treatment.
- Reduced improper payments for Medicare an estimated $15 billion since 2016 protecting taxpayer dollars and leading to less fraud, waste, and abuse.
- Took rapid action to combat antimicrobial resistance and secure access to life-saving new antibiotic drugs for American seniors, by removing several financial disincentives and setting policies to reduce inappropriate use.
- Launched new online tools, including eMedicare, Blue Button 2.0, and Care Compare, to help seniors see what is covered, compare costs, streamline data, and compare tools available on Medicare.gov.
- Provided new Medicare Advantage supplemental benefits, including modifications to help keep seniors safe in their homes, respite care for caregivers,

non-opioid pain management alternatives like therapeutic massages, transportation, and more in-home support services and assistance.

- Protected Medicare beneficiaries by removing Social Security numbers from all Medicare cards, a project completed ahead of schedule.
- Unleashed unprecedented transparency in Medicare and Medicaid data to spur research and innovation.

Remaking the Federal Judiciary

Appointed a historic number of Federal judges who will interpret the Constitution as written.

- Nominated and confirmed over 230 Federal judges.
- Confirmed 54 judges to the United States Courts of Appeals, making up nearly a third of the entire appellate bench.
- Filled all Court of Appeals vacancies for the first time in four decades.
- Flipped the Second, Third, and Eleventh Circuits from Democrat-appointed majorities to Republican-appointed majorities. And dramatically reshaped the long-liberal Ninth Circuit.

Appointed three Supreme Court justices, expanding its conservative-appointed majority to 6-3.

- Appointed Justice Neil Gorsuch to replace Justice Antonin Scalia.
- Appointed Justice Brett Kavanaugh to replace Justice Anthony Kennedy.
- Appointed Justice Amy Coney Barrett to replace Justice Ruth Bader Ginsburg.

Achieving a Secure Border

Secured the Southern Border of the United States.

- Built over 400 miles of the world's most robust and advanced border wall.
- Illegal crossings have plummeted over 87 percent where the wall has been constructed.
- Deployed nearly 5,000 troops to the Southern border. In addition, Mexico deployed tens of thousands of their own soldiers and national guardsmen to secure their side of the US-Mexico border.
- Ended the dangerous practice of Catch-and-Release, which means that instead of aliens getting released into the United States pending future hearings never to be seen again, they are detained pending removal, and then ultimately returned to their home countries.
- Entered into three historic asylum cooperation agreements with Honduras, El Salvador, and Guatemala to stop asylum fraud and resettle illegal migrants in third-party nations pending their asylum applications.
- Entered into a historic partnership with Mexico, referred to as the "Migrant Protection Protocols," to safely return asylum-seekers to Mexico while awaiting hearings in the United States.

Fully enforced the immigration laws of the United States.

- Signed an executive order to strip discretionary Federal grant funding from deadly sanctuary cities.
- Fully enforced and implemented statutorily authorized "expedited removal" of illegal aliens.
- The Department of Justice prosecuted a record-breaking number of immigration-related crimes.
- Used Section 243(d) of the Immigration and Nationality Act (INA) to reduce the number of aliens coming from

countries whose governments refuse to accept their nationals who were ordered removed from the United States.

Ended asylum fraud, shut down human smuggling traffickers, and solved the humanitarian crisis across the Western Hemisphere.

- Suspended, via regulation, asylum for aliens who had skipped previous countries where they were eligible for asylum but opted to "forum shop" and continue to the United States.
- Safeguarded migrant families, and protected migrant safety, by promulgating new regulations under the Flores Settlement Agreement.
- Proposed regulations to end the practice of giving free work permits to illegal aliens lodging meritless asylum claims.
- Issued "internal relocation" guidance.
- Cross-trained United States Border Patrol agents to conduct credible fear screenings alongside USCIS (United States Citizenship and Immigration Services) adjudication personnel to reduce massive backlogs.
- Streamlined and expedited the asylum hearing process through both the Prompt Asylum Claim Review (PACR) and the Humanitarian Asylum Review Process (HARP).
- Launched the Family Fraud Initiative to identify hundreds of individuals who were fraudulently presenting themselves as family units at the border, oftentimes with trafficking children, in order to ensure child welfare.
- Improved screening in countries with high overstay rates and reduced visa overstay rates in many of these countries.

- Removed bureaucratic constraints on United States consular officers that reduced their ability to appropriately vet visa applicants.
- Worked with Mexico and other regional partners to dismantle the human smuggling networks in our hemisphere that profit from human misery and fuel the border crisis by exploiting vulnerable populations.

Secured our Nation's immigration system against criminals and terrorists.

- Instituted national security travel bans to keep out terrorists, jihadists, and violent extremists, and implemented a uniform security and information-sharing baseline all nations must meet in order for their nationals to be able to travel to, and emigrate to, the United States.
- Suspended refugee resettlement from the world's most dangerous and terror-afflicted regions.
- Rebalanced refugee assistance to focus on overseas resettlement and burden-sharing.
- 85 percent reduction in refugee resettlement.
- Overhauled badly-broken refugee security screening process.
- Required the Department of State to consult with states and localities as part of the Federal government's refugee resettlement process.
- Issued strict sanctions on countries that have failed to take back their own nationals.
- Established the National Vetting Center, which is the most advanced and comprehensive visa screening system anywhere in the world.

Protected American workers and taxpayers.

- Issued a comprehensive "public charge" regulation to ensure newcomers to the United States are financially self-sufficient and not reliant on welfare.
- Created an enforcement mechanism for sponsor repayment and deeming, to ensure that people who are presenting themselves as sponsors are actually responsible for sponsor obligations.
- Issued regulations to combat the horrendous practice of "birth tourism."
- Issued a rule with the Department of Housing and Urban Development (HUD) to make illegal aliens ineligible for public housing.
- Issued directives requiring Federal agencies to hire United States workers first and prioritizing the hiring of United States workers wherever possible.
- Suspended the entry of low-wage workers that threaten American jobs.
- Finalized new H-1B regulations to permanently end the displacement of United States workers and modify the administrative tools that are required for H-1B visa issuance.
- Defended United States sovereignty by withdrawing from the United Nations' Global Compact on Migration.
- Suspended Employment Authorization Documents for aliens who arrive illegally between ports of entry and are ordered removed from the United States.
- Restored integrity to the use of Temporary Protected Status (TPS) by strictly adhering to the statutory conditions required for TPS.

Restoring American Leadership Abroad

Restored America's leadership in the world and successfully negotiated to ensure our allies pay their fair share for our military protection.

- Secured a $400 billion increase in defense spending from NATO (North Atlantic Treaty Organization) allies by 2024, and the number of members meeting their minimum obligations more than doubled.
- Credited by Secretary General Jens Stoltenberg for strengthening NATO.
- Worked to reform and streamline the United Nations (UN) and reduced spending by $1.3 billion.
- Allies, including Japan and the Republic of Korea, committed to increase burden-sharing.
- Protected our Second Amendment rights by announcing the United States will never ratify the UN Arms Trade Treaty.
- Returned 56 hostages and detainees from more than 24 countries.
- Worked to advance a free and open Indo-Pacific region, promoting new investments and expanding American partnerships.

Advanced peace through strength.

- Withdrew from the horrible, one-sided Iran Nuclear Deal and imposed crippling sanctions on the Iranian Regime.
- Conducted vigorous enforcement on all sanctions to bring Iran's oil exports to zero and deny the regime its principal source of revenue.
- First president to meet with a leader of North Korea and the first sitting president to cross the demilitarized zone into North Korea.

- Maintained a maximum pressure campaign and enforced tough sanctions on North Korea while negotiating denuclearization, the release of American hostages, and the return of the remains of American heroes.
- Brokered economic normalization between Serbia and Kosovo, bolstering peace in the Balkans.
- Signed the Honk Kong Autonomy Act and ended the United States' preferential treatment with Hong Kong to hold China accountable for its infringement on the autonomy of Hong Kong.
- Led allied efforts to defeat the Chinese Communist Party's efforts to control the international telecommunications system.

Renewed our cherished friendship and alliance with Israel and took historic action to promote peace in the Middle East.

- Recognized Jerusalem as the true capital of Israel and quickly moved the American Embassy in Israel to Jerusalem.
- Acknowledged Israel's sovereignty over the Golan Heights and declared that Israeli settlements in the West Bank are not inconsistent with international law.
- Removed the United States from the United Nations Human Rights Council due to the group's blatant anti-Israel bias.
- Brokered historic peace agreements between Israel and Arab-Muslim countries, including the United Arab Emirates, the Kingdom of Bahrain, and Sudan.
- In addition, the United States negotiated a normalization agreement between Israel and Morocco, and recognized Moroccan Sovereignty over the entire Western Sahara, a position with long standing bipartisan support.
- Brokered a deal for Kosovo to normalize ties and establish diplomatic relations with Israel.

- Announced that Serbia would move its embassy in Israel to Jerusalem.
- First American president to address an assembly of leaders from more than 50 Muslim nations, and reach an agreement to fight terrorism in all its forms.
- Established the Etidal Center to combat terrorism in the Middle East in conjunction with the Saudi Arabian Government.
- Announced the Vision for Peace Political Plan – a two-state solution that resolves the risks of Palestinian statehood to Israel's security, and the first time Israel has agreed to a map and a Palestinian state.
- Released an economic plan to empower the Palestinian people and enhance Palestinian governance through historic private investment.

Stood up against Communism and Socialism in the Western Hemisphere.

- Reversed the previous Administration's disastrous Cuba policy, canceling the sellout deal with the Communist Castro dictatorship.
- Pledged not to lift sanctions until all political prisoners are freed; freedoms of assembly and expression are respected; all political parties are legalized; and free elections are scheduled.
- Enacted a new policy aimed at preventing American dollars from funding the Cuban regime, including stricter travel restrictions and restrictions on the importation of Cuban alcohol and tobacco.
- Implemented a cap on remittances to Cuba.
- Enabled Americans to file lawsuits against persons and entities that traffic in property confiscated by the Cuban regime.
- First world leader to recognize Juan Guaido as the Interim President of Venezuela and led a diplomatic

coalition against the Socialist Dictator of Venezuela, Nicolas Maduro.

- Blocked all property of the Venezuelan Government in the jurisdiction of the United States.
- Cut off the financial resources of the Maduro regime and sanctioned key sectors of the Venezuelan economy exploited by the regime.
- Brought criminal charges against Nicolas Maduro for his narco-terrorism.
- Imposed stiff sanctions on the Ortega regime in Nicaragua.
- Joined together with Mexico and Canada in a successful bid to host the 2026 FIFA World Cup, with 60 matches to be held in the United States.
- Won bid to host the 2028 Summer Olympics in Los Angeles, California.Colossal Rebuilding of the Military

Colossal Rebuilding of the Military

Rebuilt the military and created the Sixth Branch, the United States Space Force.

- Completely rebuilt the United States military with over $2.2 trillion in defense spending, including $738 billion for 2020.
- Secured three pay raises for our service members and their families, including the largest raise in a decade.
- Established the Space Force, the first new branch of the United States Armed Forces since 1947.
- Modernized and recapitalized our nuclear forces and missile defenses to ensure they continue to serve as a strong deterrent.
- Upgraded our cyber defenses by elevating the Cyber Command into a major warfighting command and

by reducing burdensome procedural restrictions on cyber operations.

- Vetoed the FY21 National Defense Authorization Act, which failed to protect our national security, disrespected the history of our veterans and military, and contradicted our efforts to put America first.

Defeated terrorists, held leaders accountable for malign actions, and bolstered peace around the world.

- Defeated 100 percent of ISIS' territorial caliphate in Iraq and Syria.
- Freed nearly 8 million civilians from ISIS' bloodthirsty control, and liberated Mosul, Raqqa, and the final ISIS foothold of Baghuz.
- Killed the leader of ISIS, Abu Bakr al-Baghdadi, and eliminated the world's top terrorist, Qasem Soleimani.
- Created the Terrorist Financing Targeting Center (TFTC) in partnership between the United States and its Gulf partners to combat extremist ideology and threats, and target terrorist financial networks, including over 60 terrorist individuals and entities spanning the globe.
- Twice took decisive military action against the Assad regime in Syria for the barbaric use of chemical weapons against innocent civilians, including a successful 59 Tomahawk cruise missiles strike.
- Authorized sanctions against bad actors tied to Syria's chemical weapons program.
- Negotiated an extended ceasefire with Turkey in northeast Syria.

Addressed gaps in American's defense-industrial base, providing much-needed updates to improve the safety of our country.

- Protected America's defense-industrial base, directing the first whole-of-government assessment of our manufacturing and defense supply chains since the 1950s.
- Took decisive steps to secure our information and communications technology and services supply chain, including unsafe mobile applications.
- Completed several multi-year nuclear material removal campaigns, securing over 1,000 kilograms of highly enriched uranium and significantly reducing global nuclear threats.
- Signed an executive order directing Federal agencies to work together to diminish the capability of foreign adversaries to target our critical electric infrastructure.
- Established a whole-of-government strategy addressing the threat posed by China's malign efforts targeting the United States taxpayer-funded research and development ecosystem.
- Advanced missile defense capabilities and regional alliances.
- Bolstered the ability of our allies and partners to defend themselves through the sale of aid and military equipment.
- Signed the largest arms deal ever, worth nearly $110 billion, with Saudi Arabia.

Serving and Protecting Our Veterans

Reformed the Department of Veterans Affairs (VA) to improve care, choice, and employee accountability.

- Signed and implemented the VA Mission Act, which made permanent Veterans CHOICE, revolutionized the

VA community care system, and delivered quality care closer to home for Veterans.

- The number of Veterans who say they trust VA services has increased 19 percent to a record 91 percent, an all-time high.
- Offered same-day emergency mental health care at every VA medical facility, and secured $9.5 billion for mental health services in 2020.
- Signed the VA Choice and Quality Employment Act of 2017, which ensured that veterans could continue to see the doctor of their choice and wouldn't have to wait for care.
- During the Trump Administration, millions of veterans have been able to choose a private doctor in their communities.
- Expanded Veterans' ability to access telehealth services, including through the "Anywhere to Anywhere" VA healthcare initiative leading to a 1000 percent increase in usage during COVID-19.
- Signed the Veterans Affairs Accountability and Whistleblower Protection Act and removed thousands of VA workers who failed to give our Vets the care they have so richly deserve.
- Signed the Veterans Appeals Improvement and Modernization Act of 2017 and improved the efficiency of the VA, setting record numbers of appeals decisions.
- Modernized medical records to begin a seamless transition from the Department of Defense to the VA.
- Launched a new tool that provides Veterans with online access to average wait times and quality-of-care data.
- The promised White House VA Hotline has fielded hundreds of thousands of calls.
- Formed the PREVENTS Task Force to fight the tragedy of Veteran suicide.

Decreased veteran homelessness, improved education benefits, and achieved record-low veteran unemployment.

- Signed and implemented the Forever GI Bill, allowing Veterans to use their benefits to get an education at any point in their lives.
- Eliminated every penny of Federal student loan debt owed by American veterans who are completely and permanently disabled.
- Compared to 2009, 49 percent fewer veterans experienced homelessness nationwide during 2019.
- Signed and implemented the HAVEN Act to ensure that Veterans who've declared bankruptcy don't lose their disability payments.
- Helped hundreds of thousands of military service members make the transition from the military to the civilian workforce, and developed programs to support the employment of military spouses.
- Placed nearly 40,000 homeless veterans into employment through the Homeless Veterans Reintegration Program.
- Placed over 600,000 veterans into employment through American Job Center services.
- Enrolled over 500,000 transitioning service members in over 20,000 Department of Labor employment workshops.
- Signed an executive order to help Veterans transition seamlessly into the United States Merchant Marine.

Making Communities Safer

Signed into law landmark criminal justice reform.

- Signed the bipartisan First Step Act into law, the first landmark criminal justice reform legislation ever passed to reduce recidivism and help former inmates successfully rejoin society.

- Promoted second chance hiring to give former inmates the opportunity to live crime-free lives and find meaningful employment.
- Launched a new "Ready to Work" initiative to help connect employers directly with former prisoners.
- Awarded $2.2 million to states to expand the use of fidelity bonds, which underwrite companies that hire former prisoners.
- Reversed decades-old ban on Second Chance Pell programs to provide postsecondary education to individuals who are incarcerated expand their skills and better succeed in the workforce upon re-entry.
- Awarded over $333 million in Department of Labor grants to nonprofits and local and state governments for reentry projects focused on career development services for justice-involved youth and adults who were formerly incarcerated.

Unprecedented support for law-enforcement.

- In 2019, violent crime fell for the third consecutive year.
- Since 2016, the violent crime rate has declined over 5 percent and the murder rate has decreased by over 7 percent.
- Launched Operation Legend to combat a surge of violent crime in cities, resulting in more than 5,500 arrests.
- Deployed the National Guard and Federal law enforcement to Kenosha to stop violence and restore public safety.
- Provided $1 million to Kenosha law enforcement, nearly $4 million to support small businesses in Kenosha, and provided over $41 million to support law enforcement to the state of Wisconsin.

- Deployed Federal agents to save the courthouse in Portland from rioters.
- Signed an executive order outlining ten-year prison sentences for destroying Federal property and monuments.
- Directed the Department of Justice (DOJ) to investigate and prosecute Federal offenses related to ongoing violence.
- DOJ provided nearly $400 million for new law enforcement hiring.
- Endorsed by the 355,000 members of the Fraternal Order of Police.
- Revitalized Project Safe Neighborhoods, which brings together Federal, state, local, and tribal law enforcement officials to develop solutions to violent crime.
- Improved first-responder communications by deploying the FirstNet National Public Safety Broadband Network, which serves more than 12,000 public safety agencies across the Nation.
- Established a new commission to evaluate best practices for recruiting, training, and supporting law enforcement officers.
- Signed the Safe Policing for Safe Communities executive order to incentive local police department reforms in line with law and order.
- Made hundreds of millions of dollars' worth of surplus military equipment available to local law enforcement.
- Signed an executive order to help prevent violence against law enforcement officers.
- Secured permanent funding for the 9/11 Victim Compensation Fund for first responders.

Implemented strong measures to stem hate crimes, gun violence, and human trafficking.

- Signed an executive order making clear that Title VI of the Civil Rights Act of 1964 applies to discrimination rooted in anti-Semitism.
- Launched a centralized website to educate the public about hate crimes and encourage reporting.
- Signed the Fix NICS Act to keep guns out of the hands of dangerous criminals.
- Signed the STOP School Violence Act and created a Commission on School Safety to examine ways to make our schools safer.
- Launched the Foster Youth to Independence initiative to prevent and end homelessness among young adults under the age of 25 who are in, or have recently left, the foster care system.
- Signed the Trafficking Victims Protection Reauthorization Act, which tightened criteria for whether countries are meeting standards for eliminating trafficking.
- Established a task force to help combat the tragedy of missing or murdered Native American women and girls.
- Prioritized fighting for the voiceless and ending the scourge of human trafficking across the Nation, through a whole of government back by legislation, executive action, and engagement with key industries.
- Created the first-ever White House position focused solely on combating human trafficking.

Cherishing Life and Religious Liberty

Steadfastly supported the sanctity of every human life and worked tirelessly to prevent government funding of abortion.

- Reinstated and expanded the Mexico City Policy, ensuring that taxpayer money is not used to fund abortion globally.
- Issued a rule preventing Title X taxpayer funding from subsiding the abortion industry.
- Supported legislation to end late-term abortions.
- Cut all funding to the United Nations population fund due to the fund's support for coercive abortion and forced sterilization.
- Signed legislation overturning the previous administration's regulation that prohibited states from defunding abortion facilities as part of their family planning programs.
- Fully enforced the requirement that taxpayer dollars do not support abortion coverage in Obamacare exchange plans.
- Stopped the Federal funding of fetal tissue research.
- Worked to protect healthcare entities and individuals' conscience rights – ensuring that no medical professional is forced to participate in an abortion in violation of their beliefs.
- Issued an executive order reinforcing requirement that all hospitals in the United States provide medical treatment or an emergency transfer for infants who are in need of emergency medical care—regardless of prematurity or disability.
- Led a coalition of countries to sign the Geneva Consensus Declaration, declaring that there is no international right to abortion and committing to protecting women's health.
- First president in history to attend the March for Life.

Stood up for religious liberty in the United States and around the world.

- Protected the conscience rights of doctors, nurses, teachers, and groups like the Little Sisters of the Poor.
- First president to convene a meeting at the United Nations to end religious persecution.
- Established the White House Faith and Opportunity Initiative.
- Stopped the Johnson Amendment from interfering with pastors' right to speak their minds.
- Reversed the previous administration's policy that prevented the government from providing disaster relief to religious organizations.
- Protected faith-based adoption and foster care providers, ensuring they can continue to serve their communities while following the teachings of their faith.
- Reduced burdensome barriers to ensure Native Americans are free to keep spiritually and culturally significant eagle feathers found on their tribal lands.
- Took action to ensure Federal employees can take paid time off work to observe religious holy days.
- Signed legislation to assist religious and ethnic groups targeted by ISIS for mass murder and genocide in Syria and Iraq.
- Directed American assistance toward persecuted communities, including through faith-based programs.
- Launched the International Religious Freedom Alliance – the first-ever alliance devoted to confronting religious persecution around the world.
- Appointed a Special Envoy to monitor and combat anti-Semitism.
- Imposed restrictions on certain Chinese officials, internal security units, and companies for their

complicity in the persecution of Uighur Muslims in Xinjiang.

- Issued an executive order to protect and promote religious freedom around the world.

Safeguarding the Environment

Took strong action to protect the environment and ensure clean air and clean water.

- Took action to protect vulnerable Americans from being exposed to lead and copper in drinking water and finalized a rule protecting children from lead-based paint hazards.
- Invested over $38 billion in clean water infrastructure.
- In 2019, America achieved the largest decline in carbon emissions of any country on earth. Since withdrawing from the Paris Climate Accord, the United States has reduced carbon emissions more than any nation.
- American levels of particulate matter – one of the main measures of air pollution – are approximately five times lower than the global average.
- Between 2017 and 2019, the air became 7 percent cleaner – indicated by a steep drop in the combined emissions of criteria pollutants.
- Led the world in greenhouse gas emissions reductions, having cut energy-related CO_2 emissions by 12 percent from 2005 to 2018 while the rest of the world increased emissions by 24 percent.
- In FY 2019 the Environmental Protection Agency (EPA) cleaned up more major pollution sites than any year in nearly two decades.
- The EPA delivered $300 million in Brownfields grants directly to communities most in need including investment in 118 Opportunity Zones.

- Placed a moratorium on offshore drilling off the coasts of Georgia, North Carolina, South Carolina, and Florida.
- Restored public access to Federal land at Bears Ears National Monument and Grand Staircase-Escalante National Monument.
- Recovered more endangered or threatened species than any other administration in its first term.

Secured agreements and signed legislation to protect the environment and preserve our Nation's abundant national resources.

- The USMCA guarantees the strongest environmental protections of any trade agreement in history.
- Signed the Save Our Seas Act to protect our environment from foreign nations that litter our oceans with debris and developed the first-ever Federal strategic plan to address marine litter.
- Signed the Great American Outdoors Act, securing the single largest investment in America's National Parks and public lands in history.
- Signed the largest public lands legislation in a decade, designating 1.3 million new acres of wilderness.
- Signed a historic executive order promoting much more active forest management to prevent catastrophic wildfires.
- Opened and expanded access to over 4 million acres of public lands for hunting and fishing.
- Joined the One Trillion Trees Initiative to plant, conserve, and restore trees in America and around the world.
- Delivered infrastructure upgrades and investments for numerous projects, including over half a billion dollars to fix the Herbert Hoover Dike and expanding funding for Everglades restoration by 55 percent.

Expanding Educational Opportunity

Fought tirelessly to give every American access to the best possible education.

- The Tax Cuts and Jobs Act expanded School Choice, allowing parents to use up to $10,000 from a 529 education savings account to cover K-12 tuition costs at the public, private, or religious school of their choice.
- Launched a new pro-American lesson plan for students called the 1776 Commission to promote patriotic education.
- Prohibited the teaching of Critical Race Theory in the Federal government.
- Established the National Garden of American Heroes, a vast outdoor park that will feature the statues of the greatest Americans to ever live.
- Called on Congress to pass the Education Freedom Scholarships and Opportunity Act to expand education options for 1 million students of all economic backgrounds.
- Signed legislation reauthorizing the D.C. Opportunity Scholarship program.
- Issued updated guidance making clear that the First Amendment right to Free Exercise of Religion does not end at the door to a public school.

Took action to promote technical education.

- Signed into law the Strengthening Career and Technical Education for the 21st Century Act, which provides over 13 million students with high-quality vocational education and extends more than $1.3 billion each year to states for critical workforce development programs.

- Signed the INSPIRE Act which encouraged NASA to have more women and girls participate in STEM and seek careers in aerospace.
- Allocated no less than $200 million each year in grants to prioritize women and minorities in STEM and computer science education.

Drastically reformed and modernized our educational system to restore local control and promote fairness.

- Restored state and local control of education by faithfully implementing the Every Student Succeeds Act.
- Signed an executive order that ensures public universities protect First Amendment rights or they will risk losing funding, addresses student debt by requiring colleges to share a portion of the financial risk, and increases transparency by requiring universities to disclose information about the value of potential educational programs.
- Issued a rule strengthening Title IX protections for survivors of sexual misconduct in schools, and that – for the first time in history – codifies that sexual harassment is prohibited under Title IX.
- Negotiated historic bipartisan agreement on new higher education rules to increase innovation and lower costs by reforming accreditation, state authorization, distance education, competency-based education, credit hour, religious liberty, and TEACH Grants.

Prioritized support for Historically Black Colleges and Universities.

- Moved the Federal Historically Black Colleges and Universities (HBCU) Initiative back to the White House.

- Signed into law the FUTURE Act, making permanent $255 million in annual funding for HBCUs and increasing funding for the Federal Pell Grant program.
- Signed legislation that included more than $100 million for scholarships, research, and centers of excellence at HBCU land-grant institutions.
- Fully forgave $322 million in disaster loans to four HBCUs in 2018, so they could fully focus on educating their students.
- Enabled faith-based HBCUs to enjoy equal access to Federal support.

Combatting the Opioid Crisis

Brought unprecedented attention and support to combat the opioid crisis.

- Declared the opioid crisis a nationwide public health emergency.
- Secured a record $6 billion in new funding to combat the opioid epidemic.
- Signed the SUPPORT for Patients and Communities Act, the largest-ever legislative effort to address a drug crisis in our Nation's history.
- Launched the Initiative to Stop Opioid Abuse and Reduce Drug Supply and Demand in order to confront the many causes fueling the drug crisis.
- The Department of Health and Human Services (HHS) awarded a record $9 billion in grants to expand access to prevention, treatment, and recovery services to States and local communities.
- Passed the CRIB Act, allowing Medicaid to help mothers and their babies who are born physically dependent on opioids by covering their care in residential pediatric recovery facilities.

- Distributed $1 billion in grants for addiction prevention and treatment.
- Announced a Safer Prescriber Plan that seeks to decrease the amount of opioids prescriptions filled in America by one third within three years.
- Reduced the total amount of opioids prescriptions filled in America.
- Expanded access to medication-assisted treatment and life-saving Naloxone.
- Launched FindTreatment.gov, a tool to find help for substance abuse.
- Drug overdose deaths fell nationwide in 2018 for the first time in nearly three decades.
- Launched the Drug-Impaired Driving Initiative to work with local law enforcement and the driving public at large to increase awareness.
- Launched a nationwide public ad campaign on youth opioid abuse that reached 58 percent of young adults in America.
- Since 2016, there has been a nearly 40 percent increase in the number of Americans receiving medication-assisted treatment.
- Approved 29 state Medicaid demonstrations to improve access to opioid use disorder treatment, including new flexibility to cover inpatient and residential treatment.
- Approved nearly $200 million in grants to address the opioid crisis in severely affected communities and to reintegrate workers in recovery back into the workforce.

Took action to seize illegal drugs and punish those preying on innocent Americans.

- In FY 2019, ICE HSI seized 12,466 pounds of opioids including 3,688 pounds of fentanyl, an increase of 35 percent from FY 2018.

- Seized tens of thousands of kilograms of heroin and thousands of kilograms of fentanyl since 2017.
- The Department of Justice (DOJ) prosecuted more fentanyl traffickers than ever before, dismantled 3,000 drug trafficking organizations, and seized enough fentanyl to kill 105,000 Americans.
- DOJ charged more than 65 defendants collectively responsible for distributing over 45 million opioid pills.
- Brought kingpin designations against traffickers operating in China, India, Mexico, and more who have played a role in the epidemic in America.
- Indicted major Chinese drug traffickers for distributing fentanyl in the U.S for the first time ever, and convinced China to enact strict regulations to control the production and sale of fentanyl.

[https://trumpwhitehouse.archives.gov/trump-administration -accomplishments/]

{Author's Note: We have begun BUILDING THE WALL. Republicans want STRONG BORDERS and NO CRIME. Democrats want OPEN BORDERS which equals MASSIVE CRIME. Although President Trump accomplished a massive amount during his presidency, he also added trillions of dollars to our deficit. This is one of the reasons many of the leaders in the Senate fought him in passing much of his legislation.

What does this have to do with a book that is about the Progressive Movement? It seems this is what had to be done to stop the progressive movement. All democrats and a lot of Republicans did not like it since President Trump who was elected in 2016 was not being paid by lobbyists. Many politicians got wealthy from lobbyists which is what President Trump meant by wanting to clean out the swamp. He was a person who did not need the job of being President; his personal wealth at the time was $10 billion and some say that by being President he lost some of that wealth. He even donated his Presidential salary to *the military wounded soldiers. He put the American people first which no politician had done for decades. Not a lot from either party, Republican or Democrat, was published about the increase that these programs and increase in the economy did to the deficit. Although Trump, being a Republican, did do his share in increasing the deficit by trillions.}*

CHAPTER 12

Joe Biden - Where are We Going?

As of this writing a new president was elected who defeated President Trump and was challenged by President Trump and many of the Republicans. With Joe Biden as President, the country will be put in the path of progressiveness once again. What will the people of the country do with more debt and more regulations?

Upon taking office, on his first day in office, President Biden sat down with a bunch of executive orders to change just about everything that President Trump had put in place that created the strong economy during the 4 years of the Trump Administration. It included:

1. Killing the Key Stone pipeline
2. Completely eliminated the immigration in the Southern border which had the immigration under control
3. Stopped the construction of the border wall along the Southern border
4. Put the U.S. back in the World Health Organization which did not want to admit that China was behind the Coronavirus
5. Put the U.S. back in the Paris climate accord which the U.S. had to pay most of it.

{Autho'rs Note: This is but a few of the executive order Biden did the first day to put the U.S. back on the track of being more of a socialist society.

Throughout this book I have been calling government handouts "Entitlement", but this is not entirely true. Entitlement should not include Social Security and Medicare. Social Security is earned by an individual over the years of paying in and Medicare is paid for by the Social Security recipient through his Social Security benefit. Basically, what we have been talking about is government handouts through welfare programs. Recipients of these welfare programs refer to it as entitlement because they feel they are entitled to those free benefits from the government.

So, if the government pays out more than it takes in what can happen? It's not much different than if you ran your household the way the government runs itself. As of this writing the deficit is approaching $28 trillion and more is wanted by the Democratic congress. Presently, President Biden is pushing for a $3.5 trillion program which he will call a "Reconstruction" program.

- *Bankruptcy could occur – when you continue spending and not taking in the amount of money to pay for what you are buying, and you have to borrow to pay for what you are buying, it will finally catch up with you and you will lose it all through bankruptcy. The United States cannot continue printing money and letting other sources - such as China - buy our bonds. They will eventually own us.*
- *Your reputation would diminish along with your ability to buy anything. A reputation takes years to build up and when it is lost it could result in never getting it back.*
- *You would lose your credit score and your ability to purchase for years ahead. For individuals, this means lowering or losing your Equifax score or, in the case of the U.S. government, it means having its credit score lowered by the World Bank.*

The United States has reached a deficit spending of over $28 trillion as of 2021. The debt is now much larger than the economy itself. Obama added more $9 trillion from 2008 to the end of his term, which is more than one-third of the total debt and has seen one of the largest debt expansions in the history of the U.S. This expansion is credited primarily to his expansion of the welfare programs where over 37% (based on National Televise figures) of the American people are getting some form of welfare or government aid. Obama also overspent the country into the largest debt explosion in U.S. history. And recently, with a pandemic virus spreading and the country closing down, more assistance is needed by the population.

To give you an idea of how bad this debt it; let us take a look at just one of the $28 trillion dollars your family is responsible for and what it means to your family. How many of us have even an idea of how much or what a trillion dollar is or even what a billion is. To give you an idea, no one person has ever accumulated a trillion dollars' worth of wealth. That is why we have a hard time understanding the country's $28 trillion dollar debt.

The problem is that for the U.S. government this trillion-dollar figure is not so abstract. The government, in its overspending of the budget, intentionally overspends more than these trillion dollars each year.

In the Obama years and his running into his sixth year as president he had intentionally spent over the trillion-dollar mark; to accumulate over $7 trillion in deficit spending.

These trillions were on top of the Stimulus and after bailing out hundreds of banks, General Motors, Chrysler, AIG, Fannie Mae and Freddie Mac, which consisted of 2/3 of American mortgages. Then the Federal Reserve's and the government took over the student loan industry, and it rammed the ObamaCare down the American public's throats, who overwhelmingly was against it. This was a government grab which, if eventually is not repealed, will add trillions of more dollars to the deficit. The reason for this is that ObamaCare covers more than one sixth of the U.S. economy.

The following quote by Thomas Jefferson, taken from the

Jefferson biography by Joseph Ellis and which every American should read, *Jefferson says,*

"I place economy among the first and most important virtues, and public debt as the greatest of changes to be feared....To preserve our independence, we must not let our rulers load us with perpetual debt....We must make our choice between economy and liberty or profusion and servitude.'

{*Author's Note: With Obama's spending on welfare, the Government entitlement programs were spending well over one trillion a year during his Presidency, which is almost 40% of a budget of approaching 4 trillion dollars. To give you an idea what a trillion dollar is; if you spent one dollar per second around the clock it would take you 31,688 years to spend a trillion dollars. The Government, in spending these trillion of dollars over the years has spent money that has not yet even been earned by your children and grandchildren, by an estimated 16 trillion dollars.*

You didn't overspend the $16 trillion. Our Government did. But you and your families are now on the hook for it all. So how long will it take you to pay for all of their overspending?}

- To pay back one million dollars, at a rate of one dollar per second, would take you 11.5 days.
- To pay back one billion dollars, at a rate of one dollar per second, would take you 32 years.
- To pay back one trillion dollars, at a rate of one dollar per second, would take you 31,688 years.

The median American household income is about $50,000 per year. That translates to less than one tenth of one cent per second.

So, if your family earns $50,000 per year, and if you spend none of that on food, rent, transportation, income tax or even pursuing your own happiness, and if you take all of your family's household income and use it — not to pay down the government's current debt, but just to pay down the $1 trillion in new debt that the government overspends each year – it would take your family

32 million years to pay for it. Now, multiply that by 16 – because the government is now $16 trillion in debt – to see how long it will take for you to pay it back. That's five hundred and twelve million years. Yes, 512,000,000 years.

[https://www.foxnews.com/opinion/how-long-will-it-take-us-to-pay-back-16-trillion-in-debt]

{*Author's Note: This is scary and most families who go to the polls to vote don't understand this and officials running for office do not even touch it. Why, because most of them cause it.*

Somewhere, somehow, Washington has to return to sanity. The voters have to start paying closer attention to who they are putting in office and not let them stay in office forever if they are not looking out for the voters. The question is -- will we ever be able to pay back this kind of debt. Eventually the country, the United States and its citizens, will pay the price. And that price is closer than most Americans think.

It is interesting to note that in his book "American Spirit" about Thomas Jefferson; Joseph J. Ellis stated that Thomas Jefferson felt that the United States would only last 150 years. In his book he stated that the Jefferson Era of thinking began declining with four different occurrences. All these are based on the Progressive Movement.

The above, in discussing the deficit and the spending in this county was defined to let the readers know that Joe Biden, and his path of wanting to spend, will create a deficit that this county cannot recuperate from}

CHAPTER 13

What We Have Now

The United States will either survive this last century of Progressiveness by someone with a different political philosophy getting elected to office, or continue along a path of becoming a socialistic country with a government controlling everything we do. Or the population will listen to the final voice of the Republican Party, which still believes in the Jeffersonian philosophy of government. The problem is that right-wing conservatives are in the minority. What will it take to turn the country around? How far to the middle does the Right have to move to get into office to change things? The Republican Party needs the independent and moderate voting blocs in American to achieve this change in government. This bloc is unpredictable. I also believe that many Democrats feel the same way: that for the country to change and be more conservative in its spending it needs to look at itself and where the money is going and how much is being wasted.

As the population increased in the United States, the population became more dependent on the government. There seems to be no understanding that the more the government gives, the more the citizens become subjects or even slaves of the Washington big government establishment. The feeling that your neighbor or your local government is the answer to all of your financial issues should not exist in the 21st century in order for you to survive.

It has always bewildered me, in my studies in Organizational Behavioral Psychology, how the population will succumb to an individual such as Hitler, Stalin etc. The progressive movement in the U.S. isn't attributable to anyone individual, but rather to a Progressive Movement that started with Woodrow Wilson and ramped up through Barack Obama's term and continues up to Joe Biden's presidency. It is as if the individual loses his ability to think and act for himself. That person becomes a subject and lose the "Free Will" that God has so graciously given us as the greatest gift to mankind.

With my education in Behavioral Science and having studied Maslow, Skinner, Watson and most of all a lot of Freud, it seems that the independence we enjoyed in our life and the control we had on ourselves is being given up to the slave masters in Washington. In my last book, "Success through Behavioral Change," I explained and demonstrated how and what an individual has to do to succeed in life. In his attitude and faith in himself, in order to succeed, a person has to be able to think for himself and have a dream or vision in life to where he wants to be. With the Progressive movement, and now especially the Democratic Party, the individual is told he doesn't have to think, work or take care of himself; the government will do it for him, which takes away the individual's dream or vision of what he can do for himself. The Progressive Movement has taken away the integrity, ambition, and the self-respect the individual once enjoyed and cherished.

When will we hit the end of the Progressive Movement which takes the United States deeper into a Socialistic Government? As more Progressive politicians are elected, the more socialistic the United States becomes. What bewilders me, and I am sure many other conservatives, is how Democrats, or any politician who has been in office for 30 or even 40 years, cannot see what has happened to the country, and how the $28 Trillion in debt is hurting the economy, our credit standing in the world and our ability to trade effectively with the rest of the world.

SUMMARY

This book was written basically for my own curiosity about what has happened to America. Being raised in the 50's and 60's and understanding what we had then versus what we have now, is mind boggling. You could argue that all the rules and regulations were done for our protection, and some are, but where does the government stop controlling our lives? It seems as if, as we continue living our daily lives, the American citizen will have the government in every phase of their life. I believe it is close to that now when the government wants companies to pay for birth control. That's NOT the government's job. That is the INSURANCE company's job!

Total tax percentage potentially paid by the well above average US citizen in 2005 - 53.2%. Where is this money going except to fund the massive government progressive movement of paying the citizens to do nothing but collect food stamps, housing assistance, living expense and even cell phones. There are 10 major effects of higher taxes and the problem is that most Americans do not understand this or don't want to face the facts of what they do to the economy. The 10 effects are

1.   INADEQUATE INCOMES

The total outcome of all of the effects listed below is a large tax burden. And only workers feel the brunt of this burden, because only workers create wealth. When all of these effects are combined, the tax burden on the average worker is currently about 73 percent of income. So people can't live on their incomes.

2. LOW WAGES

Multiple governments levy so many taxes on businesses that "taxes" is the highest budget items on the ledger sheets of most businesses. These taxes take away some of the money otherwise used to pay wages. So employers can't pay good wages. *{Author's Note: Even as wages to go up the individual taxes go up leaving still less for an individual to survive on.}*

3. HIGH PRICES

Multiple governments levy so many taxes on businesses that "taxes" is the highest budget items on the ledger sheets of most most businesses. Businesses have to raise prices to get money to pay these taxes. So product prices go up. This leads to inflation. *{Author's Note: Even with automation it seems that prices continue to inflate. Buying a Chevrolet Impala in 1964 would cost approx. $1,800. In today's market an Impala would cost well over $30,000}*

4. SHODDY PRODUCTS

Multiple governments levy so many taxes on businesses that "taxes" is the highest budget items on ledger sheets of most businesses. These taxes take away money otherwise used to improve quality. Instead, businesses must cut corners to make the products and pay the high taxes. Many recalls are the results of businesses cutting too many corners, to save money so they can pay the high taxes. *{Author's Note: This is verified by an automobile company recalling millions of vehicles at one time. In 2014 62 million vehicles were recalled in the U.S. as recorded by the N.Y. Times.}*

5. PRODUCT UNAVAILABILITY AND DISCONTINUATION

Because high taxes cost businesses more, they can't provide as many products as they used to be able to. Property taxes make it expensive to stock products with lower quantities demanded. And manufacturers can't afford to produce the low-demand products and also pay their taxes. The result is that people with allergies to the mainstream products can't buy any products they can use.

6. LOST JOBS

Many businesses go bankrupt, because they can't afford to operate after government takes its cut. Other businesses flee the country, to escape the high taxes. And still other businesses must cut their payrolls to stay within their incomes. The result in each case is the loss of jobs those businesses provided in the economy.

7. FORECLOSURES, EVICTIONS, AND HOMELESSNESS

Because taxes are so high, people who originally entered into mortgages or rental contracts with the ability to pay them now no longer have the money to pay the monthly payments. Landlords also can't pay their taxes and their mortgages, causing the loss of the rental units. And if the taxes are not paid instead, the government quickly seizes the property and sells it at auction at a sheriff's sale. Thus, high taxes cause foreclosures and evictions.

With the foreclosure or eviction comes homelessness, because these victims of government greed can no longer afford to pay rent or mortgage payments. So high taxes cause homelessness. *{Author's Note: Whether the 2008 crisis was caused by the Bush administration, or the Obama economic programs is not important. It is believed that the banking policy of that time was the major cause where loans were given to many individuals* *who did not have the income to support the mortgages since most were ARM mortgages and required a balloon payment or refinance after "x" number of years. However, most people were denied the refinance because the interest rates would have been lower and the banks thought they would be losing money by refinancing at a lower rate fixed mortgage.}*

8.   POVERTY AND HIGH CRIME

Because more people can't afford to live on their incomes, the poverty rate goes up. This causes an additional drain on the budgets of government social programs. This means that each poor person can't get enough to live on.

Many poor people, unable to find jobs because government overtaxed the economy, turn to crime to get the money needed to support their families. This causes the crime rate to go up. And since many of those crimes are robberies, the violent crime rate goes up too.

9.   CHRONIC RECESSION *{Author's Note: this misspelling is verbatim from the article}*

The high taxation takes so much away from the economy that it enters a permanent form of recession. If government tries to boost the economy with increased government spending, the result is stagflation (simultaneous high inflation and unemployment) instead of prosperity. The only cure for stagflation is to cut both taxes and government spending. But this takes time to happen, keeping the effects of over-taxation in place for a time after the over-taxation ends. *{Author's Note: This is why government spending that exists from FDR and LBJ spending is still being felt in today's economy.}*

10.   LOW REAL TAX REVENUES

The permanent recession and losses of jobs caused by the high taxes cause a drop in government revenue, as economic production drops. If government then raises tax rates to recoup the lost revenue, production drops again, and the revenue drops even more. In addition to this, the increase in prices caused by the increased taxation prevents government spending from purchasing as much. So high tax rates cause lower real tax revenue collection.

{*Author's Note: Many in government do not realize that not increasing taxes and giving people more income stimulates the economy. This was a good example in the Reagan economy and the tax cuts by Trump which helped lower the unemployment to 3.5% which was the lowest in many decades.*}

Government causes its own revenue shortages by wanting more money than it should have - a victim of its own greedy ways. The size of government is naturally limited by the size of the economy around it. Attempts to make government larger than this limit causes economic trouble.

Stop asking for more from government. You will regret getting what you asked for.

[midimagic.sgc-hosting.com/taxefect.htm]

What it comes down to is this: do the citizens of the United States want to live under a socialistic type of government as is being experienced in Europe? Or is there going to be an awakening with what is happening under any socialistic president, and they finally realize they are not getting what they were promised. Instead, they are getting the following with the socialism:

1. Our school are about 26th in the world ranking for education.
2. The average family income has decreased in the past years until Trump became president, when the average income rose by approx. $6000 per year with the tax cuts and wage increases in companies.

3. The unemployment picture is the indication of how the economy is doing. Many say the increase in the Dow Jones is benefiting only the rich, since they own most of the stocks. But it has to be understood that, in a capitalistic economy, it is the rich that created the jobs - not the government.
4. Welfare would skyrocket to a point that no one knows what the accurate numbers are. Prior numbers were quoted in previous chapters.
5. Welfare costs have skyrocketed into the billions instead of the millions it was before Obama. Again, numbers were previously quoted.
6. Health insurance cost has skyrocketed under ObamaCare. While it was promised that Americans could keep their own insurance and costs would go down $2500.00 per family per year, just the opposite happened; cost went up and some people had to change both insurance providers and medical providers
7. A stimulus program was given to Obama in excess of $780 million. Roads were supposed to be repaired, schools upgraded, economies would change by increasing employment and many other promises were made. None came true: it was more of his political promises or lies to help create more socialism.

Many other items can be quoted but that would take another book. The point is: this is the result of anyone's socialistic type of programs that even Hillary Clinton, if she had been elected, would not change or be any different than what Obama's programs were. Although this writing is geared toward the situation the United States faced in 2014 and the election of 2016 it is apparent that it would and can apply anywhere in the future.

{Author's Note: So in what direction do we go: American, Socialism or the Freedom that our forefathers fought so hard for and promised the Americans?}

ABOUT THE AUTHOR

The author was born in Feb. 1943 in Ft. Fairfield, Maine and was one of seven children. This area of the country at the time (during World War II and the Korean War) was a time of just surviving. His father worked on an Air Force Base repairing B-25 bombers after their mission into Germany across Greenland, and his mother was a stay-at-home mom taking care of the 7 children, which more than kept her busy. Being brought up with 6 other children in the family gave the author the advantage of understanding what it was like to get along with others and what needed to be done to "get his way," especially since he was in the middle of the 7 children. Through school he was a loner, spending a lot of time just walking through the woods with his 22 rifle and not wanting to be around people. The reason for this is that his stuttering was so bad that he often had trouble holding a conversation - even with his own family. This made school a very difficult situation for him, which resulted in a personality that was not very controllable.

After graduating from High School in 1961 he went into the Army National Guard (6 months active duty). He was made a squad leader where, just a short time before, he would never have been considered to have any type of leadership ability. So it showed that when he was finally away from his environment he started to excel, which brought to his attention years later what kind of affect a change in environment had on an individual. He not only achieved squad leader in his company in his army training time, but the change in the environment seemed to also have an effect on his personality, resulting in more confidence, and the stuttering started to fade and eventually disappeared.

From the Army, he went on to get his Associates in Applied Science in Mechanical Technology. From there, he earned a B. S. in Industrial Technology, then his M.S. in Organizational Behavioral Science. In his college years, Ralph took as many public speaking courses as possible and, with a lot of faith, got his stuttering under control. It isn't only the education that helped him, but he strongly believes it was his change in environment and getting away from his area of childhood that made a tremendous difference. It is also strongly believed that if Ralph had stayed in his past environment not much would have changed in his life.

It was his last degree that created a curiosity in the area of human behavioral patterns, along with his own personal change that occurred in his life from changing his own environment. From this, he went on work in the field of engineering for a short time, which led him into management. In this arena he was able to use his curiosity to observe people in their work environment, and their behavior. In doing so, the author used the studies from behavioral scientists (such as B.F. Skinner, Dr. James Watson, Abraham Maslow and Sigmund Freud) to give him more knowledge and understanding of individuals and their behavioral patterns and why they acted they way they did.

Later in life, he got involved in a network marketing organization which was based totally on individuals' performances and their personalities and wanting to change their environment to fulfill their dreams. This organization led him to read other great authors on personalities, such as Robert Schuler and Dr. Norman Vincent Peale. He also spent a lot of time studying the books written by Napoleon Hill, such as "Think and Grow Rich", "The Master Key to Riches" and "Success through a Positive Mental Attitude." In this network organization he started to wonder why people got involved in a business and yet did not succeed. People higher in the organization kept saying you needed a "Dream", but what they didn't consider was that the individuals had a past environment, and recruiting the individual into the business was not enough to eliminate the past environment. Therefore, the past environment blocked their belief of ever achieving any more than what they felt they deserved. The Dream never became a reality and they never allowed themselves to believe in the Dream. This situation was never addressed by the organization.

Ralph spent 8 years with the Kiwanis Club, three of these as an officer, and one as its President. He spent 14 years with a political conservative party as its Public Relations person for setting up fund raising events. He served on the Southington High School Building committee for 8 years and 4 of these years as the Chairman of the Board of Education Advisory Committee. In that capacity, he wrote different reports on the educational growth of the community and its effect on the curriculum. Ralph has also been very active in church organizations, such as serving on church councils, and different committees within the Men's Club in the church.

He spent time teaching college to students who, by state standards, were underprivileged. More important, he also taught classes to students from Personnel Departments who needed to know more about personnel policies and how to deal with employees who had different circumstances with their employment.

It was at this time that the author decided that his thesis for his M.S. (conflict having positive results, when managed properly) should be put into a book to show that positive conflict in a person's environment can result in not only a change in the environment but help an individual to move on to achieve his or her goals in life. This book is not based just on theory, but on actual cases experienced by the author.

His experience in the management field included being a supervisor at Pratt & Whitney Aircraft where he had individuals reporting to him that were twice his age. From there, he worked at Fafnir Bearing where his worked eventually got him promoted to Manufacturing Project Engineer. His greatest knowledge of individuals came with his many years at O. F. Mossberg, a gun manufacturer, where his experience in managing over 100 individuals made him start thinking more about why people do what they do, so he decided to go on to get an M.S. in Organizational Behavioral Science.

After achieving his M.S., Ralph continued to work on his own by starting a display company and doing consulting wherever he could find a consulting job. However, his experience in a network or MLM business got him to question more about individuals and why they wouldn't perform or would not believe in themselves and believe they deserved more than what they had.

Having spent 23 years on the Republican town committee in Southington, Connecticut as a committee person, I got involved in many campaigns, whether passing out flyers on candidates or public speaking and calling many individuals on the phone. I have experienced many individuals' feelings about politics and politicians. In that time period I also campaigned and ran for a seat on the Planning and Zoning Committee.

I was also the Southington Campaign Coordinator for state 6th Congressional District for Gene Migliaro who was a State Representative. I campaigned for Gene in Southington and assisted the Town Committee on many campaigns and in the Governor's race when Gov. Rowland ran for office.

I also served on the Central Connecticut Environmental Committee, which was an appointment by the town committee, and was the lead person on many fund raisers for the town's Republican Party.

I Served on the High School Building Committee for 7 years. This was an appointed position by the Town Committee as a reward for the work that I had been doing and because they knew that I would serve the committee with the integrity that the party wanted.

I was in Kiwanis for twelve years and served as its President for two years. I also served as the New England Membership Director. In this position I traveled throughout New England getting to know and understand how people felt about their country and what it should stand for.

In my church, I served in positions on the bingo committee, as an usher, and many duties in the men's club. I am presently very involved in my church as Chairman of the Business Network, with the Men's Club and an officer for the Knights of Columbus.

This book is written from many years of past experience in town committee politics, and social and church committee experiences, along with my Master's in Organizational Behavioral Science from the University of Hartford, and most of all remembering the 50's and 60's and how wonderful and free we were without a lot of government interference.

The Progressive information was taken off the web and from other sources that I have read in the past. No one would have all this information in their own mind but in their library of information.

BIBLIOGRAPHY

Pages 5:
Webster's Dictionary

Page 6-7:
Congressional Budget Office

Page 11:
BRIA 23 1 b Progressives and the Era of Trustbusting—Constitutional Rights Foundation – Bill of Rights in Action (Spring of 2007 Volume 23, No.1

Page 16:
Theodore Roosevelt Biography, Wikipedia, the free encyclopedia

Page 19:
The Heritage Foundation – "Woodrow Wilson: Godfather of Liberalism" July 31, 2012

Page 20-21:
Wikipedia: Social Programs in the United States

Page 23-26:
Michael Barone's Book "The Almanac of American Politics".

Page 28:
Theodore Roosevelt Biography, Wikipedia, the free encyclopedia

Page 28-30:
Progressive Party (United States, 1912, the free encyclopedia
Page 30-38:
The Promise of American Life by Herbert Croly

Page 38-39:
The American Yawp Reader: Theodore Roosevelt on "The New Nationalism" (1910)

Pages 41-46:
Wikipedia's History of Woodrow Wilson

Page 47:
"The Life in the White House" by Alda D Donald

Page 48:
"What is Income" – from a Truth-Attack article

Page 50-52:
Fourteen Points – National World War I Museum and Memorial

Page 53: T
Taken from Quizlet Chapter 33

Page 54-56:
"Causes of the Great Depression – Hackensackschools.org

Page 58-59:
By Mario Rizzo Guest blogger, September 20, 2010, ThinkMarkets

Page 59-60:
Google.com – "FDR's Response to the Great Depression – Overview of a New Deal

Page 61-69:
ThoughtCo – 7 New Deal Programs Still in Effect Today

Page 72:
Quzlet.com – Chapter 30

Page 73:
Wikipedia: New Frontier

Page 78:
Kennedy's Presidential Library and Museum

Page 78-108:
Wikipedia – New Frontier

Page 112:
Wikipedia: Great Society

Page 117:
UVA Miller Center.org – Lyndon B. Johnson: Domestic Affairs

Page 118-122:
ushistory.org

Page 129-130:
https://www.nytimes.com/1994/03/30/us/clinton-wages-a-quiet-war-against-poverty.html

Page 136:
https://www.britannica.com/biography/Bill-Clinton/Presidency

Page 142:
Statistics from Facttank News in Numbers

Page 142:
"2016: Obama's America - Dinesh D'Souza (Director), John Sullivan (Director)"

Page 143:
These figures were taken from the 2013 White House Fact Sheet

Page 145:
Stephen Dinan - The Washington Times - Thursday, October 18, 2012

Page 145:
Statistics from Facttank News in Numbers

Page 147:
By Stephen Dinan - The Washington Times - Thursday, October 18, 2012

Page 153: *https://m.washingtontimes.com/news/2012/oct/18/welfare-spending-jumps-32-percent-four-years/*

Page 155:
https://www.americanprogress.org/issues/healthcare/news/2020/03/23/482012/10-ways-aca-improved-health-care-past-decade/

Page 156-157:
https://tylerpaper.com/opinion/editorials/doctor-shortages-will-limit-access/article_277fdafc-4acf-5214-8fb4-8193d8f5793c.html

Page 157:
https://www.investors.com/politics/editorials/doctor-shortages-obamacare-ehr/

Page 162:
[https://www.carolinacoastonline.com/news_times/opinions/editorials/article_574cf49e-d2b8-11e6-8960-ab7b13d83409.html]

Pages 165-256:
https://trumpwhitehouse.archives.gov/trump-administration-accomplishments/

Page 262-263:
Jefferson biography by Joseph Ellis

Page 264:
https://www.foxnews.com/opinion/how-long-will-it-take-us-to-pay-back-16-trillion-in-debt
Page 275: *[midimagic.sgc-hosting.com/taxefect.htm]*

Page 275:
midimagic.sgc-hosting.com/taxefect.htm

Printed in the United States
by Baker & Taylor Publisher Services